Ph/c

Celtic Xn

CELT, DRUID AND CULDEE

CELT, DRUID AND CULDEE

BY

ISABEL HILL ELDER

(MERCH O LUNDAIN DERRI)

LONDON

THE COVENANT PUBLISHING CO., LTD.

6 Buckingham Gate, S.W.1

1938

Celt, Druid and Culdee
First Published 1938

This reprint published 1992 by

The Banton Press
Nelson St, Largs
Scotland.

ISBN: 1 85652 126 5

"The fact that claims to some noble lineage, and also to other matters, as just and well founded, always becomes known somehow or other, even if people try to conceal it; being like musk, which spreads its odour, although it be hidden."

Abu Raihan Muhammad (Albiruni) A.D. 973-1048.

"Adventure on, for from the littlest clue
Has come whatever worth man ever knew."
Masefield.

CONTENTS

FOREWORD

BY

Admiral Cuthbert Cayley, C.B.

Mrs. Elder's work, *Celt, Druid and Culdee,* is a most valuable addition to any library.

The mass of documented evidence is a fitting answer to much that has hitherto passed as historical scholarship.

It was with much diffidence that I acceded to the author's request to write a Foreword in her publication, but the material she has gathered together from so many sources has proved a delight to me.

I am confident it will also be a delight to all who peruse the pages of her book.

An additional pleasure lies in front of me in recommending her painstaking work to all and sundry.

PREFACE

FROM a mass of material in which is intermixed legend, tradition, native history and the contributions of Greek and Roman writers to our ancient history, I have endeavoured to create within the compass of this small volume a more favourable impression of the past of the British Isles than that which is customarily received.

Fragmentary though the evidence may be of an early British civilisation and culture, and a flourishing British Church, it should go far to stimulate sympathetic appreciation of those early ancestors whose untiring efforts in defence of country and religion resulted in a heritage for us British people of freedom and humanitarian principles.

There are many perversions of truth relative to the past which the British people have long since settled down to believe, with the result that the modern sceptic hastens to cover with the chilling mantle of disbelief any attempt to present a true account of early British affairs.

It may be said that intense patriotism has obscured to my view many imperfections in the character and practices of our ancestors; the creation of this impression, however, is almost impossible to avoid when one undertakes the defence of ancient peoples. So much that belittles and even defames the early

Briton and exalts everything Roman has been written, and so little that presents an opposite view, that it seems unlikely the average reader will realise that our ancestors were neither barbarous nor idolatrous.

It has become a commonplace, in writing or conversing on the subject of the origin of religion and culture in these islands, to assume that it began about the beginning of the Roman occupation, that the early inhabitants contributed nothing, that, in fact, the conditions which prevailed prior to the arrival of the Romans were such as would obtain among the lowest type of aboriginal savages. This unworthy mental attitude is the effect of a series of causes which began with the transmutation of Roman war propaganda into history.

I undertook the study of early Christianity in our islands from a keen desire to ascertain how much we really do owe to the Romans in matters ecclesiastical as well as civil, and in the hope that it might be possible to illuminate in some degree the obscurity which enshrouds this portion of our ancient story.

In the following chapters I have tried to show that the Church came into being in a country with great features, national and political, and a great inheritance. To say that, in Britain, there were four ascending steps to Protestantism—William the Conqueror, Edward III, Wycliff, and the Reformation—is to state but a part of the truth, and robs us of a thousand years' history of a struggle for Protestantism by which the four recognised ascending steps were made possible.

The rise and establishment of Christianity in Britain has been dealt with by so many writers that one hesitates to add yet another volume to a subject which has, admittedly, definite limitations in public interest. I venture to hope, however, that in these pages it will be found that new light has been thrown on the origin of the Culdees, with whom rests the introduction, propagation, and with their successors, the defence of Apostolic Christianity brought by these first Christians to this land shortly after the Ascension of Our Lord.

My very sincere thanks are due to the Very Rev. R. G. S. King, M.A., Dean of Derry, for suggestions in research connected with the Culdees, and to others for help and suggestions, and I would especially record my indebtedness to the Rev. R. F. Guy Waddington, M.A., for his kindness in correcting the manuscript.

I. H. E.

Chester.

CHAPTER I

THE EARLY BRITONS

IT has been said that the only excuse for writing a book is that one has something to say which has not been said before. That this claim can not be made on behalf of this little volume will be very evident to the reader as he proceeds, since it is a compilation from a variety of sources from which evidence has been brought together to support the belief that the civilisation of the early Britons was of a high standard, and that they did not deserve that contempt with which they have been treated by many historians, nor the odious names of "savages" and "barbarians" by the supercilious *literati* of Greece and Rome.

When evidence, admittedly fragmentary, of the real conditions in this country from the earliest times has been brought to light throughout the centuries, it seems, almost invariably, to have been rejected in favour of Roman teaching.

In his "History of Scotland," Rev. J. A. Wylie, LL.D., says, "We have been taught to picture the earliest condition of our country as one of unbroken darkness. A calm consideration of the time and circumstances of its first peopling warrants a more cheerful view."[1] By examining the available evidence it may be possible to obtain this more cheerful view, and to show that in the darkest eras

[1] "Hist. Scot," Vol. I, p. 31.

of our country the rites of public worship were publicly observed; with this worship there were associated two ideas—a Supreme Being and life in a future state.

The popular idea that the ancestors of the British were painted savages has no foundation in fact. It was a custom of the Picts and other branches of the Gothic nations to make themselves look terrible in war, from whence came the Roman term "savage." The "painting" was in reality tattooing, a practice still cherished in all its primitive crudities by the British sailor and soldier.

Far from these ancestral Britons having been mere painted savages, roaming wild in the woods, as we are imaginatively told in most of the modern histories, they are now, on the contrary, disclosed by newly-found historical facts given by Professor Waddell[2] to have been from the very first grounding of their galley keels upon these shores, over a millennium and a half of years before the Christian era, a highly civilised and literate race, pioneers of civilisation.

The universally held belief that the British are a mixed race has prevailed during many centuries; this belief, however, is now fading out of the scientific mind and giving place to the exact opposite. Britons, Celts, Gaels, Anglo-Saxons, Danes and Normans were kinsmen, shedding kindred blood.

Freeman says, "It is difficult to realise the fact that our nation which now exists is not really a mixed

[2] "Origin of Britons, Scots and Anglo-Saxons," p. 142.

race in the sense which popular language implies."[3]

Professor Sayce, at a later date, in one of his lectures, observes that he misses no opportunity of uprooting the notion that the people who form the British nation are descended from various races; all the branches that flowed into Britain are branches of the selfsame stock. Not a single pure Saxon is to be found in any village, town or city of Germany. We once came there, but came out again in our wanderings to these British Islands.

Dr. Latham says, "Throughout the whole length and breadth of Germany there is not one village, hamlet or family which can show definite signs of descent from the Continental ancestors of the Angles of England."[4]

It is noteworthy that during the occupation of Britain by the Romans the inhabitants led a life as separate as possible from their invaders, and according to Professor Huxley, when the Romans withdrew from Britain in A.D. 410 the population was as substantially Celtic as they found it. Huxley, in 1870, in the earlier years of the Irish agitation, applied the results of his studies to the political situation in Ireland in the following words in one of his lectures: "If what I have to say in a matter of science weighs with any man who has political power, I ask him to believe that the arguments about the difference between Anglo-Saxons and Celts are a mere sham and delusion."[5]

[3] "Norman Conquest," Vol. I, Appendix A, p. 537.
[4] "Ethnology of the British Islands," p. 217.
[5] Anthrop. Rev. 1870, vol. 8, p. 197. "Forefathers and fore-runners of the British People."

The Welsh Triads and the "Chronicum Regum Pictorum" as well as the "Psalter of Cashel" give the chief early information about the inhabitants of Scotland, and all agree as to the racial unity of the different peoples, much, however, as they fought each other. This unity is recognised by Thierry,[6] Nicholas,[7] Palgrave[8] and Bruce Hannay[9] in their histories of the British people.

The Britons were renowned for their athletic form, for the great strength of their bodies, and for swiftness of foot. They excelled in running, swimming, wrestling, climbing, and all kinds of bodily exercise; were patient of pain, toil and suffering, accustomed to fatigue,[10] to bear hunger, cold and all manner of hardships. Bravery, fidelity to their word, manly independence, love of their national free institutions, and hatred of every pollution and meanness were their notable characteristics.[11]

Tacitus tells us the northern Britons were well trained and armed for war. In the battle-field they formed themselves into battalions; the soldiers were armed with huge swords and short targets; they had chariots and cavalry, and carried darts which they hurled in showers on the enemy. The cumulative evidence is of a people numerous, brave and energetic. Even Agricola could say that it were no disgrace to him, were he to fall in battle, to fall among so brave a people.[12]

[6] "Norman Conquest," p. 20.
[7] "Pedigree of the English People," pp. 58, 271.
[8] "English Commonwealth," ch. i, p. 35.
[9] "European and Other Race Origins," pp. 365, 470, 471.
[10] Pezron, "Antiq. de la Nation et de la Langue Gaulaise."
[11] See Gilbert Stone, "England from Earliest Times," p. 9.
[12] Vita Agricolæ, c. 28.

Further south similar conditions prevailed; the Romans, led by Plautius, Flavius Vespasian, the future Emperor and his brother, assailed the British, and were met with the British "stupidity" which never knows when it is beaten.

The British have been from all time a people apart, characterised by independence, justice and a love of religion. Boudicca, in her oration, as given by Dion Cassius, observes that though Britain had been for centuries open to the Continent, yet its language, philosophy and usages continued as great a mystery as ever to the Romans themselves.

The monuments of the ancient Britons have long since vanished (with the exception of Stonehenge and other places of Druidic worship), yet Nennius, the British historian, who was Abbot of Bangor-on-Dee about A.D. 860, states that he drew the greater part of his information from writings and the monuments of the old British inhabitants.[13] Our early historians were undoubtedly acquainted with a book of annals written in the vernacular tongue, which was substantially the same as the Saxon Chronicle.[14]

Nennius disclaims any special ability for the task of historian set him by his superiors, but is filled with a keen desire to see justice done to the memory of his countrymen, saying, "I bore about with me an inward wound, and I was indignant that the name of my own people, formerly famous and distinguished, should sink into oblivion and like smoke be dissipated . . . It is better to drink a wholesome draught of

[13] "Historiae Brittonum" of Nennius, Harleian M.S. 3859. (British Museum.)

[14] *Vide* Geoffrey of Monmouth, i, 1. See Cave, "Hist. Lit.," ii, 18.

B—C

truth from a humble vessel than poison mixed with honey from a golden goblet." [15]

What were once considered exaggerated statements on the part of Nennius, Geoffrey of Monmouth and other early historians are now discovered to be trustworthy. In their day these writers were regarded as historians of repute. Many of the ancient British writers were professed genealogists, men appointed and patronised by the princes of the country, who were prohibited from following other professions. [16] It was left to a later age to throw doubt on their veracity. Since it is the nature of truth to establish itself, it seems the reverse of scholarly to disregard the evidence of ancient reports embodied in the Welsh Triads and the writings of early British historians.

Milton says: "Those old and inborn names of successive kings, never to have been real persons or done in their lives at least some part of what so long hath been remembered cannot be thought without too strict incredulity." [17]

A great deal of history so-called has come down to us from Latin sources, whose one object was, from the very first, to make us believe that we owe all to Rome, when, in fact, Rome owes a great deal to us; so much error has been taught in our schools concerning the ancient Britons that it is difficult for the average student to realise that the British before the arrival of Julius Caesar were, in all probability, among the most highly educated people on the earth

[15] Nennius, "Hist. of the Britons," trans. J. A. Giles, Prol., p. 2.
[16] Gir. Camb.,"Cambriae Descript.," cap.xviii, Anglica Hibernica, ed. Camden, p. 890.
[17] "Hist. of England" (8vo.), p. 11.

at that time, and as regards scientific research surpassed both the Greeks and Romans—a fact testified to by the Greek and Roman writers themselves.[18] In all the solid essentials of humanity our British ancestors compare to great advantage with the best eras of Greece and Rome.

Lumisden has shown in his treatise on the "Antiquities of Rome" that many of the fine actions attributed by Roman historians to their own ancestors are mere copies from the early history of Greece.[19]

It is unfortunate for posterity that the histories from which modern historians have drawn their information were written by hostile strangers. That they have been accepted all along the centuries as true is a striking tribute to a people who, valiant in war and fierce in the defence of their rights, think no evil of their enemies. Truly has it been said that an essentially British characteristic is the swift forgetfulness of injury.

[18] Strabo, I, iv, p. 197. Mela. Pom, iii, 2, 18. Pliny, N. H., i, 30, c. i.

[19] "Antiq. of Rome," pp. 6, 7, 8.

CHAPTER II

LAWS AND ROADS

THE lawgiver Molmutius,[1] 450 B.C., based his laws on the code of Brutus, 1100. B.C.[2] He was the son of Cloton, Duke of Cornwall, referred to in ancient documents as Dyfn-wal-meol-meod, and because of his wisdom has been called the "Solomon" of Britain.

We have it from the great law authorities, and from the legal writers Fortescue and Coke,[3] that the Brutus and Molmutine laws have always been regarded as the foundation and bulwark of British liberties, and are distinguished for their clearness, brevity, justice and humanity.

The liberty of the subject, so marked a feature of British government to-day, runs from those remote times like a gold thread through all the laws and institutions in this country.

King Alfred, it is recorded, employed his scribe, Asser, a learned Welsh monk from St. David's (whom he afterwards made Abbot of Amesbury and Bishop of Sherbourne), to translate the Molmutine laws from

[1] "Ancient Laws of Cambria" (British Museum, 5805, A.A.4), Myv. Arch., Vol. II. Brut. Tysillo.
[2] Toland, "Hist. Druids," p. 230.
[3] De Laudibus Legum Angliae; Coke Preface, third vol. of Pleadings. Fortescue, "Brit. Laws," published with notes by Selden, ch. 17, pp. 38, 39.

the Celtic tongue into Latin, in order that he might incorporate them into his own Anglo-Saxon code. [4]

The following are appended as examples:

"There are three tests of Civil Liberty: equality of rights, equality of taxation, freedom to come and go.

"Three things are indispensable to a true union of nations: sameness of laws, rights, and language.

"There are three things free to all Britons: the forest, the unworked mine, the right of hunting.

"There are three property birthrights of every Briton: five British acres of land for a home, the right of armorial bearings, the right of suffrage in the enacting of the laws, the male at twenty-one, the female on her marriage.

"There are three things which every Briton may legally be compelled to attend: the worship of God, military service, and the courts of law.

"There are three things free to every man, Briton or foreigner, the refusal of which no law will justify: water from spring, river or well, firing from a decayed tree, a block of stone not in use.

"There are three classes which are exempt from bearing arms: bards, judges, graduates in law or religion. These represent God and His peace, and no weapon must ever be found in their hands.

"There are three persons who have a right to public maintenance: the old; the babe; the foreigner who cannot speak the British tongue." [5]

From time immemorial the laws and customs of

[4] Summarised by Edmund Spenser, "Faerie Queen," Book II, Stanza xxxix (ed. Morris).

[5] "Triads of Dynvall Moëlmud, ap. Walter," p. 315. Myv. Arch. Vol. III. "Ancient Laws of Cambria" ap. Palgrave and Lappenberg.

Britain differed from those of other nations, and that the Romans effected no change in this respect is very plainly set forth by Henry de Bracton, a thirteenth-century writer: "Whereas in almost all countries they use laws and written right, England alone uses within her boundaries unwritten right and custom. In England, indeed, right is derived from what is unwritten which usage has approved. There are also in England several and divers customs according to the diversity of places, for the English have many things by custom which they have not by written law, as in divers countries, cities, boroughs and vills, where it will always have to be enquired what is the custom of the place, and in what manner they who allege the custom observe the custom."[6]

Another point on which Britain differs from other countries is that she has ever maintained the Common Law which holds a person under trial innocent until proved guilty, whereas the Continental nations maintain the Civil Law, which holds him guilty until proved innocent.

Molmutius, the first king in these islands to wear a crown of gold,[7] is said to have founded the city of Bristol, which he called Caer Odor—"the city of the chasm." His son, Belinus, who succeeded him, built a city where London now stands, which he called Caer Troia, and also the first Thames Embankment. He constructed a sort of quay or port made of poles and planks and erected a water-gate. That gate, the

[6] "Legibus et Consuet." pp. 4, 5.
[7] Holinshed, "Chronicles," ch. xxii, p. 117. Geoffrey of Monmouth, Book II, ch. xvii.

only gate admitting into London on the south side, became Belinus Gate or Belin's Gate. [8]

Belinus lived to the age of eighty. When he died his body was burned (they did not call it cremation in those days) and his ashes were enclosed in a brazen urn, which was placed on the top of the gate; henceforth it was Belin's Gate, and it requires no undue stretch of imagination to see that Belin's Gate has become Billingsgate.

Billingsgate enjoys the proud distinction of being the first Port of London, the only Port of London at that time, and thus the men of Billingsgate became the first Port of London Authority.

Cambria Formosa, daughter of Belinus, 373 B.C., greatly promoted the building of cities. She is said to have taught the women of Britain to sow flax and hemp and weave it into cloth. Her brother, Gwrgan, first built the city of Cambridge, which he called Caer-Gwrgan.[9]

The so-called Roman roads in Britain were constructed centuries before the Romans came to these islands. The Dover to Holyhead Causeway, called Sarn Wydellin or Irish Road, later corrupted into Watling Street; the Sarn Ikin, later Icknield Street, led from London northwards through the eastern district, and Sarn Achmaen from London to Menevia (St. David's).

These were causeways or raised roads (not mere trackways, as sometimes erroneously stated), except

---

[8] E. O. Gordon, "Prehistoric London," p. 146.
[9] Lewis, "Hist of Britain," p. 52. *See* Baker's MSS. in the University Library, Cambridge, XXIV, 249.

where raised roads were impossible, and this accounts for the term "Holloway" in some parts of the country.

Our roads were begun by Molmutius and completed by his son Belinus, 400 B.C. On their completion a law was enacted throwing open these roads to all nations and foreigners. "There are three things free to a country and its borders: the river, the roads and the place of worship. These are under the protection of God and His peace." In this law originated the term "the King's Highway."[10]

Writers who maintain that the British roads were simply unmade trackways seem unaware of the fact that the British were skilled charioteers; this fact, without other evidence, should go a long way to prove that the roads of ancient Britain were hard and well made. Charioteering is not brought to perfection on soft, boggy trackways, nor are chariots built without wheelwrights and other mechanics skilled in the working of iron and wood.

Only once before, in the war with Antiochus, 192 B.C., the Romans met with similar chariots, but never in any European country. The British chariot was built after the Eastern pattern, adorned with carved figures and armed with hooks and scythes. British chariots were prized possessions of the Romans.

Diodorus Siculus, 60 B.C., states: "The Britons live in the same manner that the ancients did: they fight in chariots, as the ancient heroes of Greece are said

[10] Ancient Laws of Cambriae" (British Museum, 5805, A.A.4). Stukeley, "Abury," p. 42.

to have done in the Trojan wars. . . . They are plain and upright in their dealings, and far from the craft and subtlety of our countrymen. . . . The island is very populous. . . . The Celts never shut the doors of their houses; they invite strangers to their feasts, and when all is over ask who they are and what is their business."[11]

Britain, long before the Roman invasion, was famous for its breed of horses and the daring and accomplishment of its charioteers; and after the arrival of the Romans the large space given by their historians to the wars in Britain demonstrate the interest felt in them by the whole empire. Juvenal could suggest no news which would have been hailed by the Roman people with more satisfaction than the fall of the British king Arviragus (Caractacus):

"Hath our great enemy,
Arviragus, the car-borne British king,
Dropped from his battle-throne?"

The evidence is as strong as the nature of the subject requires that in Britain the Romans found roads made and in use for vehicular traffic; chariots, among other items, superior to their own, and the inhabitants governed by ancient native laws.

[11] Dio. Sic., Book. V, ch. x. Senchus Mor., IV, 237.

CHAPTER III

COMMERCE AND DRESS

TACITUS and Strabo describe Londinium as famous for the vast number of merchants who resorted to it for its widely-extended commerce; for the abundance of every species of commodity which it could supply, and they speak of British merchants bringing to the Seine and the Rhine shiploads of corn and cattle, iron and hides, and taking back brass, ivory and amber ornaments.[1]

That Londinium was considered by the Romans as the Metropolis of Britain is further established by the fact that it was the residence of the Vicar of Britain.[2] The abode of such an office clearly marks London as having been a seat of government, of justice, and of the administration of the finances which consequently contributed to its extent, its magnificence and its wealth.[3] Britain was, in fact, from at least 900 B.C. to the Roman invasion, the manufacturing centre of the world.

The Abbé de Fontenu proved that the Phœnicians had an established trade with Britain before the Trojan war, 1190 B.C.[4]

[1] Strabo, "Geogr." iii, 175; iv, 199.
[2] A Roman office.
[3] Amm. Marcell. Lib. xxviii, ch. 89.
[4] "Mem. de Littérature," tome VII, p. 126.

The Phœnician Admiral, Himilco of Carthage, who visited Britain about the sixth century B.C. to explore "the outer parts of Europe," records that the Britons were "a powerful race, proud-spirited, effectively skilful in art, and constantly busy with the cares of trade."[5]

The British farmer had a market for his produce beyond the shores of Britain. We learn from Zosimus that in the reign of Julian, A.D. 363, eight hundred pinnaces were built in order to supply Germany with corn from Britain.[6]

When the Romans invaded Britain in A.D. 43, they found the inhabitants in possession of a gold coinage and of beautifully-wrought shields of bronze[7] and enamelled ornaments.[8] Fine specimens of richly-enamelled horses' trappings may be seen in the British Museum, and the bronze shield found in the Thames, near Battersea, adorned with enamelled designs, Rice Holmes describes as the "noblest creation of late Celtic art."[9]

The beautiful brooches discovered in different parts of these islands clearly demonstrate that the Britons were skilful and artistic metal workers, and in the centuries of Roman domination the Celtic patterns did not die out. A peculiarly Celtic type is the "dragon" brooch, "representing a conventionalised writhing dragon, often magnificently

[5] Fragment preserved by Festus Avienus, "Ora Maritama," V, 98-100.

[6] Zosimus, Lib. III, p. 43. (Ed. Bas.)

[7] Philostratus, a Greek sophist (third century), who resided at the Court of Julia Domna, describes the British process.

[8] Gilbert Stone, "England from the Earliest Times," p. 10.

[9] "Anc. Brit.," p. 244.

inlaid with enamel and recalling in its vigorous design and curvilinear motives all the essential qualities of late Celtic art. Thus the native Celtic tradition of metal-work continued under Roman rule to flourish and to produce types which were not merely Roman, but recognisably Celtic."[10]   In a further description of these brooches Mr. Collingwood says: "In the true Celtic spirit the ornament on the trumpet head is often made with eyes and nostrils, to resemble the head of an animal; but however the brooch is finished in detail, it is almost always a masterpiece both of design and of manufacture."[11]

Enamelling was an art unknown to the Greeks till they were taught it by the Celts.[12]

Dr. Arthur Evans tells us that the Romans carried off some of the Britons to Rome to teach them the art of enamelling as well as that of glass-making.

Stukeley, giving an account of a glass urn discovered in the Isle of Ely in the year 1757, observes that the Britons were famous for glass manufacture.[13]

The early Britons were workers in pottery, turnery, smelting and glass work.[14]   In the excavations at Glastonbury well-made instruments of agriculture were found: tools, files, safety-pins, and the remains of wells and bridges.

The British tin mines were, from the earliest times, world renowned.   Diodorus Siculus says: "These

[10] R. G. Collingwood, "Roman Britain," p. 76.
[11] "Archaeology of Roman Britain," p. 253.
[12] J. Romilly Allen, "Celtic Art," p. 136.
[13] Minutes of Antiq. Soc., London, March, 1762.
[14] J. Smith, "Galic Antiq.," p. 64.

people obtain the tin by skilfully working the soil which produces it."[15] Herodotus speaks of the British Isles under the general term of Cassiterides, or the tin islands.[16]

The lead mines of Britain were worked long before the Roman occupation, and it is believed that during the partial domination of Rome the mining continued to be carried out by Celtic workmen.[17]

Dr. John Phillips, the geologist, stated in 1855 that without due consideration being given to the lead-mining industry our ideas "of the ancient British people would be altogether conjectural, derogatory and erroneous."[18]

Eumenius, A.D. 266, private secretary to Constantine Chlorus, says: "Britain is full of skilled craftsmen."[19]

The coins of ancient Britain are worthy of more than a passing notice. Numismatists tell us that our ancient British types cannot amount to much less than four hundred in number, of which possibly two hundred may have inscriptions;[20] this variety is to be accounted for by the fact that each tribe had its own stamped currency in gold, silver and bronze.

Canon Lysons says: "It is to be remembered that the earliest British coins are not imitations of the Roman coinage; they much resemble the coinage of

[15] Book V, ch. x.
[16] "Thalia," Sect. C, xv. (Bel. ed.)
[17] Gordon Home, "Roman York," p. 27.
[18] Yorks. Philos. Soc., Vol. I, p. 92.
[19] "Panegyric on Constantius," C. ii.
[20] J. Evans, "Coins of the Anc. Brit.," p. 171.

Philip of Macedon, Alexander the Great, and the Greek and Eastern mintage."[21]

Dr. Borlase, in his "Antiquities of Cornwall," asserts that the wheel under the horse intimated the making of a highway for carts, and that the wheel is common on the coins of Cunobelinus, 14 B.C.; on those of Cassebelinus, 51 B.C.; and also on the Cornish coins, which from their character appear to be older than the rest.

Sir John Evans devotes sixty-four pages of his standard work, "Ancient British Coins," to the coins of Cunobelinus and the history of his reign.

That Cunobelinus (the Cymbeline of Shakespeare) was a man of education and refinement is well borne out in his coins, universally considered to be a true index and reflection of the mind. Numismatists say that the Cunobelinus types are by no means a Roman type, and could hardly have been struck except by express command.[22]

The coins of Arviragus, son of Cunobelinus, minted at Colchester, are, where they are included, the gems of every collection.

The horse, sometimes thought to have been introduced as a national emblem by the Saxons, is one of the most common types upon the coins of the ancient Britons.

M. De la Saussaye, in describing the gold coin assigned to the Druid Abaris, mentioned by Hecatæus, says: "I have been induced to modify my assertion on more than one point, and I particularly recognise

---

[21] "Our British Ancestors," p. 41.
[22] "Coins of Cunobelinus and of the Ancient Britons," p. 26.

religious ideas peculiar to the Celts expressed on their monetary uninscribed types."[23]

The palm trees on the coins of the Southern Belgae, who settled in Kent, Sussex, Hants, Wilts, Dorset and Devon, proclaim the Eastern origin of these people.

From the modern pictorial representations of our ancestors we are expected to believe that their dress consisted of an animal skin fastened round the waist, and that they wandered, thus scantily clad, about their island home, living on nuts and berries.

Boudicca, Queen of the Iceni (the inhabitants of Norfolk and Suffolk), was described by Dion Cassius as a woman of commanding appearance. "Her stature exceeded the ordinary height of woman; her aspect was calm and collected, but her voice had become deep and pitiless. Her hair, falling in long golden tresses as low as her hips, was collected round her forehead by a golden coronet; she wore a 'tartan' dress fitting closely to the bosom, but below the waist expanding in loose folds as a gown; over it was a chlamys or military cloak. In her hand she bore a spear."[24]

In these descriptions of native dress it is interesting to note the early use of the tartan. A British hooded cloak was evidently regarded by the Romans as a superior garment, for in Diocletian's Edict of Prices, issued in A.D. 301, the price of the British cloak was the highest on the list, with the exception of the

[23] "La Revue Numismatique" for 1842, p. 165.
[24] Dion Cassius (Xiphilinus Excerpta), p. 176. *See* Strabo, Bk. IV, ch. iv, 3.

Gallic. If the price was high on account of the quality of the wool, the statement of the epigrammatist Martial, A.D. 60, is substantiated that, among other attractions, Britain was "for wool, past compare."[25]

The Britons appear to have been also importers of cloth; according to one authority, Phœnician cloths of Beyrout, once the home of our patron saint, George, were largely worn by the inhabitants of ancient Britain[26].

A torque or gold collar was worn by wealthy inhabitants, and also as a distinguishing sign of eminence.[27] Specimens of these torques have been discovered from time to time, and may be seen in various museums, notably Dublin National Museum, and in private collections. A very good example, in the possession of the Duke of Westminster and deposited at Eaton Hall, was found at Bryn Sion, Caerwys Mill: it is 32 inches long and weighs 24 ounces.

[25] Martial, Lib.I, ep. 32, and Lib. III, ep. 20.
[26] Rev. Canon Parfit, M.A., "St. George of Merry England" (1917).
[27] Gibson's "Camden," p. 653. Hoare, "Ancient Wilts," Vol. I, p. 202.

CHAPTER IV

THE ROMAN INVASION

At the time of the Roman invasion sufficient evidence of prosperity and culture existed in Britain to arouse the admiration of the invaders, and it is a matter of history that the inhabitants of these islands led a life as separate as possible from them.

It was only after ten years incessant warfare that the Romans, in A.D. 43, succeeded in effecting a footing in Britain. This is not reconcilable with the view that the Romans were invading the territory of untrained, undisciplined savages. The resistance of Britain was, in reality, against the whole of the north of Europe and was highly creditable to the brave defenders of their country.

To estimate aright the military abilities of the British general, Caswallon, and the resources of the people at the period of the first collision of our island with the Continent, it should be borne in mind that they were engaged against, perhaps, the ablest general of antiquity. The double repulsion of the Julian expedition, 55 and 54 B.C., remains un-paralleled in British history.

Tacitus reluctantly tells us that, "In Britain, after the captivity of Caradoc, the Romans were repeatedly defeated and put to the rout by the single state of the

Silures alone."[1]   The Silures, the inhabitants of south-west Britain, were noted for their military prowess and culture.

It is evident from the partial story furnished by the invaders themselves that the resistance offered by the Britons to their invaders was a surprise for which they were ill-prepared; this resistance came not from hordes of savages, but from a nation whose leaders were well versed in military tactics.   The Britons were determined to defend their ancient laws and institutions at all costs.   They evinced profound homage for the memory of their forefathers, and from their inborn love of liberty sprang the undaunted energy with which they met the mercenary and implacable plunderers of the world!   By no people was every inch of country contested with more bravery and surrendered more stubbornly than by these Britons; on terms, indeed, which rendered every victory for the Romans little better than defeat.   It is absurd to suppose that such a nation could be barbarous.

If popular amusements are to be taken as the test the Romans were themselves the most barbarous of the nations of Europe.   When the brutal sports of the gladiators were proposed to be introduced at Athens even the cynics cried out: "We must first pull down the statue to mercy which our forefathers erected fifteen hundred years ago."

A similar gulf separated the British from the Roman temper, and the comparisons of the latter people with regard to the former should be received

[1] "Annals," xii, 38, 39.

with the caution which we would exercise to-day in receiving the accounts of hostile strangers.

All the evidences supplied by Caesar refute the notion of material barbarism. Agriculture was universal, corn everywhere abundant, pasturage a distinct branch of national wealth, and the population so numerous as to excite his astonishment— "hominum multitudo infinita"—the surest and most satisfactory proof of a sound social state and ample means of sustenance.[2]

Having effected a landing (and the testimony of their own historians is that never was country more dearly purchased nor held with more difficulty), the Romans proceeded with their policy of destruction, for which they had become notorious on the continent of Europe.

One notable instance has come down to us of the Roman spirit of cruel indifference to human feelings and sufferings. The immensely wealthy Prasutagus, king of the Iceni, apprehensive, in the event of his death, of the Roman brutality likely to be experienced by his queen, Boudicca, and his two daughters, he left one half of his fortune to the Emperor Nero, endeavouring thus to secure for them a measure of protection; when, however, his death took place in A.D. 60, the Roman præfect, Caius Decius, seized the royal hoard on the pretext that it came under the denomination of public property. Resistance being made, the legionaries stormed the palace and carried the treasures off to the Castra.[3] The story of the

[2] Rev. R. W. Morgan, "St. Paul in Britain," p. 79.
[3] Tacitus, "Annals," xiv, 31.

barbarous treatment meted out to its inmates need not be repeated here. Nor of Boudicca, stung to frenzy by these atrocities, bravely taking to the field in defence of her family and her people, the Roman præfect having, in direct violation of the Claudian treaty, also confiscated the estates of many of the Icenic nobility.

Seneca, the millionaire Roman philosopher, advanced to the Iceni, on the security of their public buildings, a sum of money—about two million pounds sterling, modern—at ruinous rates;[4] this loan, suddenly and violently called in, was the indirect cause of the Boadicean war.

Boudicca, before leading her people, and the tribe of the Trinobantes who had joined them, to war, ascended the "generals' " tribunal and addressed her army of 120,000 in these words: "I rule not like Nitocris, over beasts of burden, as are the effeminate nations of the East, nor, like Semiramis, over tradesmen and traffickers, nor, like the man-woman, Nero, over slaves and eunuchs—such is the precious knowledge these foreigners introduce amongst us— but I rule over Britons, little versed indeed in craft and diplomacy, but born and trained to the game of war; men who in the cause of liberty stake down their lives, the lives of their wives and children, their lands and property. Queen of such a race, I implore your aid for freedom, for victory over enemies infamous for the wantonness of the wrongs they inflict, for their perversion of justice, for their insatiable greed; a people that revel in unmanly pleasures, whose

[4] Dion Cassius (Xiphilinus Excerpta).

affections are more to be dreaded and abhorred than their enmity. Never let a foreigner bear rule over me or over my countrymen; never let slavery reign in this island."[5]

Boudicca's many successful engagements with the Roman armies are given in our histories, and when her death took place in Flintshire, after her eventual defeat, the Romans were impressed with the extraordinary magnificence of her obsequies. According to Tacitus,[6] Boudicca died by poison; in the course of nature according to the Greek historian, Dion Cassius.

Boudicca's kinsman, Caradoc, on meeting with the Romans, displayed a like spirit of bravery and courage; perhaps, indeed, no warrior of ancient times succeeded in winning so much admiration from the enemy as this king of the south-western Britons, better known by his Latinised name of Caractacus.

The Welsh, or Cymry, as the Eldest Tribe, held three priorities. Priority as the first colonisers of Britain; priority of government; and later, priority as the first Christians of Britain.[7] From this premier tribe was to be elected the Pendragon, or military dictator, with absolute power for the time being in the case of national danger or of foreign invasion.

The king of the Cymry at the time of the Roman invasion was Arviragus (Ard an rhaig), literally king-paramount, and now elected Pendragon with the

[5] Dion Cassius (Xiphilinus Excerpta).
[6] "Annals," xiv, 37.
[7] Triads of the Cymry.

title of Caradoc[8] (Caer-vraight-tagos), literally king-commander. This Pendragon was proudly referred to by his fellow countrymen as the "Praiseworthy Opposer." Arviragus had yet another name, Gueirydd (Justiciary, from his office of administrator of justice), and by this name is mentioned in the Welsh Chronicles.

Caradoc was no rude savage, fighting out of mere animal instinct or in ignorance of the might of his adversary. Familiar with the Latin language, this king was a true representative of the higher classes of the Britons, among whom a general taste for literature, a keen susceptibility to all intellectual gratifications, a minute acquaintance with all the principles and practice of their own national jurisprudence, and a careful training in the schools of the rhetoricians, was very generally diffused. Hence the rejoicing at Rome when this military leader was betrayed and subsequently conducted through the capitol, amidst the excitement of three million inhabitants who thronged the line of procession to obtain a view of the formidable captive. The Senate was convened; the famous trial of Caradoc followed, in which, before the tribunal of the Emperor, he delivered himself thus: "Had my government in Britain been directed solely with a view to the preservation of my hereditary domains, or the aggrandisement of my own family, I might, long since, have entered this city an ally, not a prisoner; nor would you have disdained for a friend, a prince,

[8] Triad 79. Suetonius, "Caligula," ch. xliv. Tacitus, "Annals," xii, 36.

descended from illustrious ancestors, and the dictator of many nations. My present condition, stript of its former majesty, is as adverse to myself as it is a cause of triumph to you. What then? I was lord of men, horses, arms, wealth; what wonder if, at your dictation, I refused to resign them! Does it follow that because the Romans aspire to universal dominion every nation is to accept the vassalage they would impose? I am now in your power—betrayed, not conquered. Had I, like others, yielded without resistance, where would have been the name of Caradoc? Where your glory? Oblivion would have buried both in the same tomb. Bid me live. I shall survive for ever in history, one example at least of Roman clemency."[9]

The preservation of Caradoc forms a solitary exception in the long catalogue of victims to merciless policy of Imperial Rome. His life was spared on condition that he never again bore arms against Rome. After a residence of seven years in free custody in Rome he was allowed to return to Britain.

Caradoc, in maintaining his descent from illustrious ancestors, could bring from the clan records evidence of his pedigree; in those remote times genealogies were guarded with extreme care and recorded with exactitude by the herald-bard of each clan.[10] On the public reception, at the age of fifteen, of a child into the clan, his genealogy was proclaimed and challengers of it commanded to come forward.

[9] Tacitus, "Annals," xii, 37. Zonaras Annals. xi, 10, 11.
[10] "Anglica Hibernica," ed. Camden, p. 890.

Pedigree and inheritance were so identified in the ancient British code that an heir even in the ninth descent[11] could redeem at a valuation by jury any portion of an estate with which his forefathers had been compelled to part.

All the family of Caradoc were attached to literary pursuits; copies of the best Roman and Greek authors were circulated in Siluria and deposited in the chief centres of Druidic learning.[12]

Caradoc's daughter, Gladys (re-named Claudia by the Roman Emperor after her arrival in Rome with the other members of the Silurian family as hostages), wrote several volumes of hymns and odes.[13] Her praises were sung by the poet Martial:

"Our Claudia, named Rufina, sprung we know
   From blue-eyed Britons; yet behold, she vies
   In grace with all that Greece or Rome can show,
As bred and born beneath their glowing skies."

In a later epigram Martial writes:

"For mountains, bridges, rivers, churches and fair
   Women, Britain is past compare."[14]

Caradoc's sister, "Pomponia Grecina," received her cognomen through her acquaintance with Greek literature.

The state of the country of the northern Britons is indicated by the number of large cities beyond the Forth, which Agricola explored with his fleet. This

---

[11] Richard of Cirencester, Bk. I, ch. iii, note.
[12] Rev. R. W. Morgan, "St. Paul in Britain," p. 104.
[13] Collier's "Eccl. Hist.," Bk. I.
[14] Martial, iv, 13; xi, 54.

could not mean cities which he himself erected, having been only six years in the country, nor could cities have arisen in that period, "amplas civitates" as we learn from his biographer, Tacitus.

In a general account of Britain, Ptolemy, in A.D. 110, enumerates fifty-six cities; later, Marcianus, fifty-nine.

It was not until the reign of Hadrian, A.D. 120, that Britain was incorporated by treaty, not conquest, with the Roman dominions;[15] the Britons retained their kings, land, laws and rights, and accepted a Roman nucleus of the army for the defence of the realm. These local kings and princes of Britain were obliged to become lieutenants of the Roman Emperor, as the heads of our counties are now styled lieutenants of the King. They were bound to permit the construction of a Roman castra garrisoned by Roman legionaries, with their usual staff of engineers, in their chief city. On the ruins of British buildings and monuments rose the Roman castras and villas, the remains of which are treasured by many in this country who appear to be quite unaware of the earlier civilisation.

The buildings the Romans erected were foreign to British ideas and never became an integral part of British life.

When Alaric and his Goths were engaged in the sack of Rome the Britons remembered their ancient independence and their brave ancestors; and having armed themselves, they threw off the Roman yoke, deposed the imperial magistrates and proclaimed

[15] Spartians "Vita Hadriani," ch. I.

their insular independence. The Emperor Honorius sent letters addressed to the civitates of Britain, clearing them from the responsibility of being any part of the Roman world.[16]

The Romans came to a country which was in all its essentials prosperous and free. They left it in many places devastated. Roman policy is tersely summed up in the words of the Pictish sovereign, Galgacus, "To robbery, slaughter, plunder, the Romans give the lying name of Empire; they make a solitude and call it peace."[17]

The Roman imperial system had its strong points, but it had many weak ones—the two main weak points were war and slavery. With the Romans war became the instrument of progress, but it was a system fatal to real progress and to the domestic virtues. To plough the soil and wait for the harvest seemed to them a spiritless method of acquiring that which might more easily be obtained by conquest. Eloquence and the affairs of government, as well as the exciting and barbarous sports of the arena, were esteemed and valued by Rome more than religion; hence her basilicas and amphitheatres were far more spacious and magnificent than her temples.

Wilford states that the old Indians were acquainted with the British Islands, which their books describe as the sacred islands of the west, and called one of them Britashtan, or the seat or place of religious duty.[18]

[16] Zosimus, vi, pp. 376, 381. Also Du Bos, Gibbon, Procopius, Gildas and Bede.
[17] Tacitus, vita Agricolæ, xxx.
[18] "Asiatic Researches," v, 3.

The temper of the Britons may be judged by the evidence of the important part a non-idolatrous religion exercised in their daily lives; it has been said that the history of Britain is written in her churches. This truism is applicable from the most remote times, and from the nature of ancient British worship it is possible to discover the source of the uprightness, the independence and the tolerance which characterised the early Britons.

These characteristics were noted by the Romans without acting upon them as the least check to unprincipled avarice and ambition. Salvian, A.D. 430, does not hesitate to say that the barbarians (so-called) led better lives than the Romans, even of those who were orthodox. "Their modesty," he says, "purifies the earth, all stained by Roman debauchery."[19] Amid the calamities and sufferings of the first invasion of Rome by our Gothic ancestors in A.D. 402, St. Augustine of Hippo remarked upon the marvellous forbearance of the soldiers of Alaric the Goth before the tombs of the Christian martyrs; he even went so far as to speak of the mercy and humility of these terrible victors.

To British genius alone we owe the foundation of our modern civilisation, including roads, laws, learning and a culture of worldwide fame for more than two thousand years. From a more accurate knowledge of British history we shall gain some notion of that primeval liberty and self-government, common at first to the early Britons and preserved to-day by the British people.

[19] "On the Government of God."

That the Britons adopted anything they thought good from the Romans is perfectly true; they did not, however, abandon any of their old essential laws and customs, and still less their religion. But it is as untrue to say that the Britons had no previous civilisation of their own as it is to pretend that Roman laws and customs permanently established themselves in Britain and remained after the legions were withdrawn. There is sufficient evidence to prove that the ancestors of the British, centuries before the Romans gained a footing in this country, were a polished and intellectual people, skilled in arms as well as in learning, with a system of jurisprudence of their own, superior even to the laws of Rome.[20] To these early Britons we owe what we prize most—country, peace, knowledge and higher sense of right and wrong. This goodly heritage comes to us neither from a Roman conquest nor through Roman influence.

It is not, however, for the British to pride themselves as a superior race, but rather that they are a ministering race, and that through them should flow the blessings of peace and good-will to all the nations of the world.

Montalembert declares: "It is in England that the nobility of man's nature has developed all its splendour and attained its highest level. It is there that the generous passion of independence, united to the genius of association and the constant practice of self-government, have produced those miracles of fierce energy, of dauntless vigour, and obstinate

[20] John Pym Yeatman, "Early Eng. Hist.," p. 9.

heroism, which have triumphed over seas and climate, time and distance, nature and tyranny, exciting the perpetual envy of all nations, and among the English themselves a proud enthusiasm.

"Loving freedom for itself, and loving nothing without freedom. . . . Upon herself alone weighs the formidable responsibility of her history."[21]

"Love thou thy land with love far brought
From out the storied Past, and used
Within the Present, but transfused
Thro' future time by power and thought—
True love turn'd round on fixed poles,
Love, that endures not sordid ends,
For English natures, freemen, friends,
Thy brothers, and immortal souls."

Tennyson.

[21] "Monks of the West," Vol. II, pp. 366, 367.

CHAPTER V

DRUIDISM

THE popular conception of Druidism is that it was the religion of ancient Britain and nothing more. This is a very great misconception. Druidism was, in fact, the centre and source from which radiated the whole system of organised civil and ecclesiastical knowledge and practice of the country.[1]

The Order constituted its church and parliament; its courts of law, its colleges of physicians and surgeons, its magistracy and clergy. The members of the Order were its statesmen, legislators, priests, physicians, lawyers, teachers and poets.

The truth about the Druids, to be found amongst fragments of literature and in folk-memory, is that they were men of culture, well-educated, equitable and impartial in the administration of justice. These ancient leaders of thought and instruction in our islands had lofty beliefs as to the character of the one God, Creator and Preserver, and of man's high origin and destiny. They believed in the necessity for atonement for sin, in the immortality of the soul and the resurrection of the body. The British Druids believed that every existence and form of life would continue for ever—purged from evil.

[1] Ed. Davies, "Celtic Researches," pp. 171, 182.   Diogenes Laertius in proem., p. 5.

46

To reverence the Deity, abstain from evil, and behave valiantly were, according to Laertius, the three grand articles enjoined by the Druids.[2]

In Druidism the British nation had a high standard of religion, justice and patriotism presented to it, and a code of moral teaching that has never ceased to influence national character.

It has frequently been stated that the name, Druid, is derived from Drus, an oak; the oak was held by the Druids to symbolise the Almighty Father, self-existent and eternal. The idea arose from the apparent similarity of the two words, Drus and Druid, and was merely incidental. A much more likely derivation is from Druthin, a servant of Truth.[3] The motto of the Druidic Order, "The Truth Against the World," was the principle on which Druidism was based and by which it offered itself to be judged.

"It may be asked," says the Rev. Archdeacon Williams, "how has it come to pass, if great events marked the epoch between the departure of the Romans and the death of Bede, that the whole history is so obscure, and that no literary documents remain to prove the wisdom of the teachers and the docility of the people? The answer is very plain. Such documents do exist: they have been published for more than half a century, but have hitherto wanted an adequate interpreter"[4]

The published compositions of the Druids and

[2] In Proem, p. 6.
[3] Macpherson, "Dissertations," p. 341.
[4] Gomer: a Brief Analysis of the Language and Knowledge of the Ancient Cymry. London. 1854.

Bards form but a very small portion of the extant remains of their works. The Myvyrian MSS. alone, now deposited in the British Museum, amount to 47 volumes of poetry of various sizes, containing about 4,700 pieces of poetry, in 1,600 pages, besides about 2,000 epigrammatic stanzas. There are also in the same collection 53 volumes of prose, in about 15,300 pages, containing a great many curious documents on various subjects. Besides these there are a vast number of collections of Welsh MSS. in London and in private libraries in the Principality.[5]

In A.D. 383 Druidism, while accepting Christianity, "submitted to the judgment and verdict of county and nation the ancient privileges and usages; the ancient learning, sciences and memorials were confirmed, lest they should fail, become lost and forgotten—this was done without contradiction or opposition."[6]

The educational system adopted by the Druids is traced to about 1800 B.C., when Hu Gadarn,[7] or Hu the Mighty, led the first colony of Cymri into Britain from Defrobane, where Constantinople now stands.[8] In the justly celebrated Welsh Triads Hu Gadarn is said to have mnemonically systematised the wisdom of the ancestors of those people whom he led west from the summer-land. He was regarded as the personification of intellectual culture and is

[5] Matthew Arnold, "Celtic Literature," p. 254.

[6] Triodd Braint a Defod, Walter, op. cit., p. 33. Llyod's "Hist. of Cambria," ed. Powell, praef. p. 9.

[7] Myv. Arch., ii, 57.

[8] "Traditional Ann. of the Cymry," p. 27. Triad 4. Sharon Turner, "Hist. Ang. Sax." Vol. I, ch. ii, p. 38, Note 29.

commemorated in Welsh archæology for having made poetry the vehicle of memory and to have been the inventor of the Triads. To him is attributed the founding of Stonehenge and the introduction of several arts, including glass-making and writing in Ogham characters. On Hu Gadarn's standard was depicted the ox; in this possibly may be discovered the origin of the sobriquet "John Bull."

Hu established, among other regulations, that a Gorsedd or Assembly of Druids and Bards must be held on an open, uncovered grass space, in a conspicuous place, in full view and hearing of all the people.

Concerning the educational facilities available to the so-called barbarous people of these islands, there were at the time of the Roman invasion forty Druidic centres of learning, which were also the capitals of the forty tribes; of these forty known centres nine have entirely disappeared.

These forty colleges were each presided over by a Chief Druid.[9] There were also in Britain three Archdruids, whose seats were at London, York and Caerlleon-on-Usk.

The territories of the forty tribes (the originals of our modern counties) preserve for the most part the ancient tribal limits. Yorkshire, for instance, retains the same disproportioned magnitude to our other counties—the territory of the large and powerful tribe, the Brigantes.

The students at these colleges numbered at times

[9] Gildas, MS. (Julius, D.XI), Cottonian Library.   Morgan's "British Cymry."

D—c

sixty thousand of the youth and young nobility of Britain and Gaul. Caesar comments on the fact that the Gauls sent their youth to Britain to be educated. It required twenty years to master the complete circle of Druidic knowledge. Natural philosophy, astronomy, mathematics, geometry, medicine, jurisprudence, poetry and oratory were all proposed and taught—natural philosophy and astronomy with severe exactitude.[10]

Caesar says of the Druids: "They hold aloof from war and do not pay war taxes; they are excused from military service and exempt from all liabilities. Tempted by these great advantages, many young men assemble of their own motion to receive their training; many are sent by parents and relatives. Report says that in the schools of the Druids they learn by heart a great number of verses, and therefore some persons remain twenty years under training.[11] They do not think it proper to commit these utterances to writing, although in almost all other matters and in their public and private accounts they make use of Greek characters. I believe that they have adopted the practice for two reasons—that they do not wish the rule to become common property nor those who learn the rule to rely on writing, and so neglect the cultivation of the memory; and, in fact, it does usually happen that the assistance of writing tends to relax the diligence of the student and the action of memory. They also lecture on the stars

---

[10] Strabo, I, iv, p. 197. Caesar's Com. Lib. V. Suetonius, V. Caligula. E. Campion, "Account of Ireland," p. 18.

[11] See Toland's "Hist. of the Druids," p. 50.

and their motion; the magnitude of the earth and its divisions; on natural history; on the power and government of God; and instruct the youth on these subjects."[12]

While the Druids used writing for all other subjects taught in their colleges, in connection with the subject of religion they never used this medium. To the spread of Christianity we owe most of the information we possess of the Druidic religion; their secret laws gradually relaxed as they became Christian, and some of their theology was then committed to writing.

Dr. Henry, in his "History of England," has observed that collegiate or monastic institutions existed among the Druids.[13]

Caesar several times calls the Druidic institution a *disciplina*,[14] a term that implies a corporate life— organisation as well as the possession of learning. Mela speaks of the Druids as "teachers of wisdom."[15] The affirmation of Diodorus that, "some whom they call Druids, are very highly honoured as philosophers and theologians," is repeated by Hyppolytus.[16]

Not only the supreme king, but every petty king had his Druid and Bard attached to his court. This Druidic chaplain had charge of the education of the youthful members of the house, but was also allowed to have other pupils. He taught and lectured when

---

[11] De Bell. Gall. vi, 15, 16.
[13] "Hist. of Great Britain," Vol. I, ch. ii, p. 142. Amm. Marcel., "Hist.," xv, 9.
[14] De Bell. Gall., vi, 13, 14.
[15] Pompon. Mela, iii, 2, 18.
[16] Philosoph., i, 25.

possible on all appropriate occasions, often out-of-doors, and when travelling through the territory of his chief or from one territory to another his pupils accompanied him, still receiving instruction; when, however, the pupils exceeded in number that which he was entitled by law on such occasions to have accommodated as his own company at a house those in excess were almost always freely entertained by neighbours in the locality.

The chief poet appears to have been always accompanied by a number of assistants of various degrees, who had not yet arrived at the highest attainment in their profession.[17]

The theological students were given a particularly long course of training, and no Druidic priest could be ordained until he had passed three examinations in three successive years before the Druidic college of his tribe. The head of the clan possessed a veto on every ordination.[18]

By very stringent laws the number of priests was regulated in proportion to the population; and none could be a candidate for the priesthood who could not in the previous May Congress of the tribe prove his descent from nine successive generations of free forefathers. Genealogies, therefore, were guarded with the greatest care. This barrier to promiscuous admission had the effect of closing the Order almost

[17] O'Curry's "Manners and Customs of Anc. Irish," Vol.II. School of Simon Druid in O'Mulconry's Glossary: M.S.H. 2, 16 (Coll. 116), in Trinity College Library, Dublin. See also Reeve's "Adamnan," p. xlvii.

[18] Stanihurst, "De Rebus in Hibernia," p. 37.

entirely to all but the Blaenorion or aristocracy, making it literally a "Royal Priesthood."

Degrees were conferred after three, six and nine years' training. The highest degree, that of Pencerdd or Athro (Doctor of Learning), was conferred after nine years. All degrees were given by the king or in his presence, or by his licence before a deputy, at the end of every three years.[19]

Druidic physicians were skilled in the treatment of the sick; their practice was far removed from the medicine-man cult, so unfairly ascribed to them by their contemporary enemies and lightly followed ever since. They prayed to God to grant a blessing on His gifts, conscious that it should always be remembered that no medicine could be effective nor any physician successful without Divine help. The chief care of the physicians was to prevent rather than to cure disease. Their recipe for health was cheerfulness, temperance and exercise.[20] Certainly the power of physical endurance displayed by the early Britons was a strong testimony to the salutary laws of hygiene enforced and the general mode of life encouraged by the Druids.

Human bones which had been fractured and re-set by art have been found in Druidical tumuli.[21]

When Nuadha, an early Irish king, lost his hand in battle, "Creidne, an artificer, put a silver hand upon him, the fingers of which were capable of motion." Moreover, "besides possessing ships and

[19] "Book of Lecain," fol. 168. Toland, "Hist. Druids," p. 223.
[20] J. Smith, "Galic Antiq.," p. 80.
[21] S. Lysons "Our British Ancestors," p. 44.

armies and working in the metals, the Irish had an organised body of surgeons, whose duty it was to attend upon the wounded in battle; and they had also a Druid class to preserve the history of the country and the deeds of kings and heroes."[22]

Astronomers were deeply versed in every detail of their profession; classic judges of eminence, Cicero and Caesar, Pliny and Tacitus, Diodorus Siculus and Strabo, speak in high terms of the Druid astronomers.

Ammianus Marcellus, A.D. 350, says: "The Druids were men of a penetrating and subtle spirit, and acquired the highest renown by their speculations, which were at once subtle and profound. Both Caesar[23] and Mela[24] plainly intimate that they were conversant with the most sublime speculations of geometry and in measuring the magnitude of the earth."

Stonehenge, "the Greenwich observatory" and great solar clock of ancient times, was pre-eminently an astronomical circle;[25] heliograph and beacon were both used by the ancient British astronomer in signalling the time and the seasons, the result of observations for the daily direction of the agriculturist and the trader.

The unit of measure employed in the erection of Stonehenge and all other works of this nature in our islands was a cubit, the same as the Great Pyramid.[26]

[22] Ignatius Donnelly, "Atlantis," pp. 410, 411.
[23] Lib. VI.
[24] Lib. III.
[25] *Vide* Sir Norman Lockyer, "Stonehenge," 1906.
[26] Wm. Stukeley, "Stonehenge," p. 11.

The supposed magic of the Druids consisted of a more thorough knowledge than was common of some of the sciences—astronomy, for instance. Diodorus Siculus states that the Druids used telescopes—this, evidently, is the origin of the story that the Druids could, by magic, bring the moon down to the earth.

The visit of the British Druid, Abaris, who travelled extensively in Greece, was long remembered at Athens. Greek fancy transformed the magnetic needle by which he guided his travels into an arrow of Apollo which would transport him at wish whithersoever he pleased.[27]

Many of the wells on Druidic sites, known to-day as holy wells, were the old telescope wells of the Druids, connected with their astronomical observations.[28]

The old saying, "Truth lies at the bottom of a well," comes down to us from this use of wells in those remote times.

British architects trained in Druidic colleges were in great demand on the Continent. In this country the profession of architecture was legally recognised. There were three offices of chief architect,[29] the holders of which were privileged to go anywhere without restriction throughout the country, provided they did not go unlawfully.

James Fergusson, the writer of one of our best

[27] Hecat. ab. Diod. Sicul, Lib. III. Avienus, "de Britannia." Smith, "Hist. Druids," pp. 69, 70. Cartes' "Hist. Eng.," Vol. I, p. 52.

[28] Strabo, Bk. XVII, ch. i. Sir G. Cornewall Lewis, "Ast. of the Ancients," p. 198.

[29] Triad 32.

histories of architecture, says: "The true glory of the Celt in Europe is his artistic eminence, and it is not too much to assert that without his intervention we should not have possessed in modern times a church worthy of admiration, or a picture, or a statue we could look at without shame, and, had the Celts not had their arts nipped in the bud by circumstances over which they had no control, we might have seen something that would have shamed even Greece and wholly eclipsed the arts of Rome. . . . The Celts never lived sufficiently long apart from other races to develop a distinct form of nationality, or to create either a literature or policy by which they could be certainly recognised; they mixed freely with the people among whom they settled and adopted their manners and customs."[30]

C. J. Solinus, A.D. 80, in his description of Britain, mentions the hot springs of Bath and the magnificence with which the baths at that place had already been decorated for the use of bathers.[31]

The primitive religion of Britain, associated in so many minds with the worship of the heavenly bodies, was the worship of the "Lord of Hosts," the Creator of the Great Lights, the sun and moon; not the worship of the heavenly bodies themselves. The Universe was the Bible of the ancients, the only revelation of the Deity vouchsafed them. The wonders of Nature were to them as the voice of the All-Father, and by the movements of the heavenly

[30] "Hist. of Architecture," p. 73.
[31] "Monumenta Historica Britannica," p. 12.

bodies they ordered their lives, fixed religious festivals and all agricultural proceedings.

The way to Christianity for the early inhabitants of Britain was traced by Nature herself, and from Nature to Nature's God; St. Paul, in his letter to the Corinthians, says, "Howbeit that was not first which was spiritual, but that which is natural and afterwards that which is spiritual."

Lucanus, an educated Roman, fifty years after Christ, bears testimony to the simple faith of the Celtic races. "To you only it is given," he writes, "the knowledge or ignorance, whichever it may be, of the gods and the power of Heaven: your dwelling is in the lone heart of the forest. From you we learn that the bourne of man's ghost is not the pale realm of the monarch below. In another world the spirit survives still—death, if your lore be true, is just the passage to enduring life."[32]

Strabo observes that the care of worshipping the Supreme Being is great among the British nation; and the historian Hume, that no religion ever swayed the minds of men like the Druidic.[33]

It has been said that the Druidic circles cannot, in strictness, be termed temples, for the Druids taught that there were but two habitations of the Deity—the soul, the invisible—the universe, the visible. The word "temple," in its primitive meaning, is simply a place cut off, enclosed, dedicated to sacred use, whether a circle of stones, a field or a building. In the old British language a temple or sanctuary was called

[32] "Pharsalia," i, 457.
[33] "Hist. of England," Vol. I, p. 6.

a "caer," a sacred fenced enclosure. The stone circles or caers of Britain were, therefore, essentially temples and held so sacred by the people that reverent behaviour in their vicinity was universal. Joshua, it will be remembered, by God's command erected a circle at Gilgal (circle) immediately on the Chosen People's arrival in the Promised Land. The British caer has no connection with castra.

There seems, however, to be no doubt that the chambered barrows and cairns generally of Britain were used as temples; several points in their structure lead to this assumption. Mr. MacRitchie, in his "Testimony of Tradition," mentions several of these points, among them fireplaces and flues for carrying away smoke.

Sir Norman Lockyer[34] says: "Mr. Spence has pointed out the extreme improbability of Maeshowe (Orkney) being anything but a temple, and I may now add on the Semitic model. There were a large central hall and side rooms for sleeping, a stone door which could have been opened or shut from the inside and a niche for a guard, janitor or hall porter!"[35]

The great circle and temple known as Avebury ("Ambresbiri, the Holy Anointed Ones") is of special interest as the Westminster Abbey of ancient times;[36] the last resting place of princes, priests and statesmen, warriors, poets and musicians. One of the old Druids

[34] "Stonehenge," p. 254.
[35] "Standing Stones and Maeshowe of Stennes." 1894.
[36] Stukeley, "Abury," p. 40.

alluding to Avebury calls it "The Great Sanctuary of the Dominion."[37]

The circles or temples were composed of monoliths upon which the employment of metal for any purpose was not permitted. Druidic worship was without figure or sculpture of any kind.[38] The monolithic avenues, symbolic of the sun's path through the Zodiac, were in some instances seven miles long. The national religious procession moved through these to the circle on the three great festivals of the year. In several of our own cathedrals we have the signs of the Zodiac, represented as sacred emblems on the tiles of the sanctuary floor, for instance, at Canterbury and Rochester.

In his description of the temple at Jerusalem Josephus says: "The loaves on the table, twelve in number, symbolised the circle of the Zodiac."[39]

Druidic services were held while the sun was above the horizon: the performing of ceremonies at any other time was forbidden by law.[40] The Chief Druid or the Archdruid, when he was present, occupied a position by a large central stone, approaching it with a sword carried by its point to signify his own readiness to suffer in the cause of truth. This central stone, called Maen Llog, or the Stone of the Covenant, and now distinguished by the name of Cromlech, was in Ireland called "Bethel"[41] or the

[37] A. Llwyd, "Island of Mona," p. 41.

[38] Origen on "Ezekiel," Homily IV.

[39] Josephus, "Jewish Wars," Bk. V, p. 132.

[40] Myv. Arch., Vol. III (Laws of Dynwal Moelmud).

[41] Vallancy, "Collectanea de Rebus Hibernicus," p. 211. Lysons, "Our British Ancestors," p. 196.

house of God. Near to it was another, which received in a cavity water direct from the clouds. This water, and the waters of the river Dee (called Drydwy, the divine water), the Jordan of ancient Britain, were the only waters permitted to be used in Druidic sacrifices.

In the "Faerie Queen" Spenser speaks of the

". . . Dee which Britons long ygone
Did call divine, that doth by Chester tend."

For centuries after Druidism had merged into Christianity the Dee continued to be regarded a sacred river. A striking instance of folk-memory is recorded in connection with the battle of Chester, A.D. 613, when Dionoth, Abbot of Bangor, delivered an oration to the defeated Britons (who had retreated along the banks of the river) and concluded by ordering the soldiers to kiss the ground in commemoration of the body of Christ and to take up the water in their hands out of the river Dee and drink it in remembrance of His sacred blood. This act gave the men fresh courage; they met the Saxons bravely, and Ethelfrid, the Northumbrian invader, was defeated.[42]

The Bards of Britain, whose office it was to cultivate the art of music and poetry as well as literature, are referred to by Strabo as hymn-makers;[43] they were responsible for the temple music and for the conduct of the musical part of the temple

[42] King's "Vale Royal," p. 2. "Annales Cambriae," CLXIX.
[43] Strabo, "Geogr.", iv, 4, 5; xv, 1, 5. M. F. Cusack, "Hist of Ireland," p. 116, note.

services. On these occasions they wore white robes—from this custom has descended our English Church custom of clothing the choristers in white surplices. [44]

It was not until the first century A.D. that the Jews introduced the wearing of surplices into their services. Josephus says: "Now as many of the Levites as were singers of hymns persuaded the king (Agrippa) to assemble a Sanhedrim and to give them leave to wear linen garments as well as the priests; for, they said, this would be a work worthy of the times of his government, that he might have a memorial of such a novelty as being his doing; nor did they fail of obtaining their desire." [45]

Referring to Stonehenge, Hecatæus, a Greek writer, 320 B.C., says that the people living in these islands worshipped in a beautiful temple, whose minstrels hymned with their golden harps [46] the praise of the God they adored, and whose priesthood was a regular descent from father to son.

While every British subject was entitled at birth to five British (ten English) acres of land for a home in the hereditary county of his clan, priests were entitled to ten acres (twenty English); [47] exemption from combative military service; permission to pass unmolested from one district to another in time of war; maintenance when absent on duty from their home, and contribution from every plough in their district.

[44] E. Wilson, "Lights and Shadows," p. 262. Triad 233.
[45] Josephus, Ant., Book xx, 9.
[46] Dio. Sic., tom. I, p. 158. Taliesen, "Bards and Druids of Britain," Nash, p. 15.
[47] "Anc. Laws of Cambria" (British Museum).

The ceremonial dress of the Archdruid was extremely gorgeous; no metal but gold being used in any part of it. The Cymric or Tau Cross was wrought in gold down the length of the back of the robe; he wore a gold tiara and a breastplate of the same precious metal.[48]   A breastplate of this kind, very similar to that worn by the Hebrew high priest, was found in an excavated cist at Stonehenge, upon the skeleton of a British Druid.[49]   Five similar breastplates have been found in Britain and Ireland.

The Chevron Bead, a bead encased in gold, was worn by the Archdruid as a symbol of the Deity,[50] and designated by the Roman historians the "Druid's Egg," around which so much legend has been woven by the imaginative uninformed, who saw in the symbol only a talisman endowed with most magical powers.

The stories that are told and believed of human sacrifice by the Druids are pure inventions of the Romans to cover their own cruelty and to excuse it. The Druids sacrificed sheep, oxen, deer and goats: charred remains of these have been found at Avebury, Stonehenge and St. Paul's.   No trace of human sacrifice has been discovered in Great Britain.[51]

It is very generally believed that the Celts were nature worshippers, that they gave Divine honours to rivers, mountains and woods.   It is entirely a mistake

[48] Vallancy, "Collect. de Rebus Hibernicus," p. 459. Hulbert's "Religions of Ancient Britain," p. 30.

[49] Crania Britannicae, Vol. I, p. 78.

[50] See Elizabeth Wilson's "Lights and Shadows," pp. 6 7.

[51] Hulbert's "Religions of Britain," p. 37. Hen. Huntingdon, "Hist.," Lib. III apud res Anglie. Script., p. 322, ed. Saville. Lewis, "Hist. of Britain," ch. ii.

to believe that they did so. They were nature lovers—
never nature worshippers; neither had they a multitude of gods and goddesses, as is often affirmed.[52]
The gods and goddesses were mere mascots, and their
descendants are apparently no less superstitious.
Mascots and charms have lost none of their
popularity.

Other nations never obtained a proper compre-
hension of Druidism; they corrupted what they had
learned of the Druidism of Britain, blending with it
religions less pure. It is recorded by Caesar that those
in Gaul who wished to be perfectly instructed in
Druidism crossed the sea to what they believed to be
its birthplace.

In the Christian era St. Patrick used the shamrock
to instruct the people in the doctrine of the Trinity,
and in earlier days the Druids used the oak for the
same purpose. They sought a tree having two
principal arms springing laterally from the upright
stem, roughly in the form of a cross. Upon the right
branch they cut the name Yesu; upon the middle or
upright stem Taranis; upon the left branch Belenis;
over this they cut the name of God—Thau.[53] The
Hebrew prophets, it will be noted, referred to their
expected Messiah as "The Branch."

The mistletoe was another form of representation
to them of their Yesu, to whose coming they looked
forward with as great expectancy as did the Jews in
the East to their Messiah—the Britons were actually

[52] See Stukeley's "Abury," pp. 2, 38, 49, 76.
[53] Schedius, "Treatise de Mor Germ., XXIV. Thos. Maurice,
"Indian Antiquities," Vol. VI, p. 49.

in advance of the Jews, for, while the Britons believed implicitly in the immortality of the soul, many of the Jews did not.

"The Druids," writes Caesar, 54 B.C., "make the immortality of the soul the basis of all their teaching, holding it to be the principal incentive and reason for a virtuous life."[54] Pomponius Mela (A.D. 41) ascribes the bravery of the Britons to their doctrine of the immortality of the soul,[55] and Marcus Annæus Lucanus, A.D. 38, mentions their indifference to death as the result of this belief.[56]

The similarity of the Semitic and British worships has been commented on by archæologists and others who have explored megalithic remains in this country. Sir Norman Lockyer says: "I confess I am amazed at the similarities we have come across";[57] and Edward Davies: "I must confess that I have not been the first in representing the Druidical as having had some connection with the patriarchal religion."[58] William Stukeley, from a close study of the evidence, affirms: "I plainly discerned the religion professed by the ancient Britons was the simple patriarchal religion,"[59] an opinion which every critical and candid student of Druid ritual, customs and teaching must endorse.

[54] De Bell. Gall., Lib. VI, ch. xiii.

[55] Pom. Mel., Lib. III, ch. ii.

[56] Pharsalia, I, 453.

[57] "Stonehenge and Other British Monuments," p. 252.

[58] "Mythology and Rites of the British Druids as Ascertained from National Documents," pref., p. vii.

[59] "Abury," pref., p. i. G. Smith, "Religions of Ancient Britain," p. 43.

The unity of the Godhead was the very soul and centre of Druidism, and this unity was a Trinity. Procopius of Cæsarea, A.D. 530, says: "Jesus, Taran, Bel—One only God. All Druids acknowledge One Lord God alone."[60]

The indisputable fact is the Druids proclaimed to the universe, "The Lord our God is One." And when Christianity preached Jesus as God, Druidism had the most familiar name of its own Deity presented to it. In the ancient British tongue Jesus has never assumed its Greek, Latin or Hebrew form, but remains the pure Druidic Yesu. It is singular that the ancient Briton never changed the name of the God he and his forefathers worshipped, nor has he ever worshipped but one God.[61]

In the Cornish folk-lore whole sentences were treasured up (without being understood), and when written down were found to be Hebrew. One of these rendered into English is: "Lift up your heads, O ye gates, and be ye lift up, ye everlasting doors, and the King of Glory shall come in." "Who is this King of Glory? The Lord Yesu: He is the King of Glory."[62]

Druidism, with its self-evident Old Covenant origin, which latter was, in fact, the great "oral secret" transmitted by Druid sages from generation to generation; its doctrine of the Trinity; worship entirely free from idolatry; furtherance of peace and contribution to the settling of disputes among the

[60] De Gothicis, Lib. III. Origen on "Ezekiel" (Richardson's "Godwin de Presulibus").
[61] Dr. Henry, "Hist. of Great Britain," i, 2.
[62] Rev. Dr. Margoliouth "Jews in Britain," Vol. I, p. 23; Vol. III, p. 198.

laity; high moral tone; and insistence on the liberty and rights of the subject was a perfect preparation for the reception of Christianity.

Upon the introduction of Christianity the Druids were called upon, not so much to reverse their ancient faith, as to "lay it down for a fuller and more perfect revelation." No country can show a more rapid, natural merging of a native religion into Christianity than that which was witnessed in Britain in the first century A.D. The readiness with which the Druids accepted Christianity, the facility with which their places of worship and colleges were turned to Christian uses, the willingness of the people to accept the new religion, are facts which the modern historian has either overlooked or ignored.

CHAPTER VI

IRISH DRUIDS

MAGI—the Latin equivalent for Druids—was used by early Irish writers, and frequently by the Welsh; their synonymity in the modern mind appears to be almost entirely lost.[1] The term "Magi" conjures up a sacred meaning, indicative of the exact opposite to that which we have been led to believe about the Druids.

"The Druids were, in Celtic hagiology, constantly termed Magi."[2]

It is quite possible that the "Magi" of New Testament fame[3] who "departed into their own country another way" (Matt. ii, 12) visited Britain on their return journey to the East.

Tradition always bears a vein of truth; however fantastic, therein lies buried fact, and Irish historians have reiterated all along the centuries that Conor

[1] Rev. W. Hughes, "Church of the Cymry," p. 4. Rev. D. James, "Patriarchal Religion," p. 19. Holinshed, "Chronicles," p. 19. Vallancy, "Collect. de Rebus Hibernicus," pp. 454-456. "Book of Rights," p. xlix. Adamnan, "Vita S. Columbae," p. 73 (see also Reeve's note to this word). Pliny, "Nat. Hist," xvi, 43, 95. King Lachaire (fifth century) is described in the "Book of Armagh," fol. 3.b. as surrounded by his Magi.

[2] Rev. G. F. Maclear, D.D., "Conversion of the West. The Celts," p. 24.

[3] Book of Taliesen in Skenes' "Four Anc. Books of Wales," Vol. II, p. 174. Matt. ii, 1, "Feuch Tangedar Druids a naird shor go Hiarusalem" (Celtic). The Advent was prophesied by Cu Cullan, the Irish High Priest or Archdruid (Archbish. Cormac's Lexicon).

Macnessa, King of Ulster, who died A.D. 48, was made aware by his chief Druid, Bacrach, of the happenings in Palestine at the time of the Crucifixion, this king, requiring of his Druid an explanation of the darkness that was "over the earth."[4] (Luke xxiii, 44.)

It is not improbable that the Druid had his information and enlightenment as to the fulfilment of prophecy from the visiting Druids or Magi from the East. It would be perfectly natural on the part of these Magi to visit Britain, the headquarters of Druidism.

Toland, in his "History of the Druids," relates that in Ireland, as in England, the Druids were exempt from bearing arms, yet they finally determined concerning peace or war. Some of them were allied to kings, and many of them were kings' sons, and great numbers of them were drawn from the aristocracy.

They wore long habits, as did the Bards and Ovates, but the Druids wore white surplices when they religiously officiated. They, with the graduate Bards and Ovates, had the privilege of wearing six colours in their breachans or robes; the king and queen, seven; lords and ladies, five; governors of fortresses, four; officers and young gentlemen, three; soldiers, two; and common people, one. This sumptuary law most of the Irish historians say was enacted under Achaius (Eochaidh Ollamhfodla) the First, a king of the Irish 1383 B.C.[5]

---

[4] Registered by the pagan annalist, Phlegon, in his chronology of the Olympiads, Book 13 under ol. 202. 4.

[5] O'Curry, "Manners and Customs," Vol. I, p. 244.   C. O'Connor, "Diss. on Irish Hist.," p. 6.

This king also ordained that every noble person should have a coat of arms assigned him to distinguish him in battle and rally his followers. Hence the coat of arms, the crest, or cognisance often was appended to a man's name and became his surname.

The Bards were divided into three orders or degrees, namely, chronologers, heralds and poets. The first registered genealogies, the second sang the praises of great men, and the third, including inferior rhymers, lived most of the year free of cost.

In a great national assembly at Drumceat, in the County of Londonderry, under Aidus Anmireus, the eleventh Christian king, in the year 575, where were also present Adius, King of Scotland, and St. Columba, it was decreed that for the better preservation of their history, genealogies and the purity of their language, the supreme monarch and the subordinate kings, with every lord of a cantred or hundred, should entertain a poet of his own, no more being allowed by the ancient law of the island, and that upon these and their posterity a portion of land should be settled for ever. At the assembly, St. Columba pleaded for the independence of Scottish Dalriada from Irish suzerainty, and for toleration for the Irish bards, who had been banished by the king for their exactions and turbulence.[6] The inferior rhymers lived by travelling from place to place and by entertaining the people with satire and song.

It was also decreed that for the encouragement of learning among poets and antiquaries public schools

[6] Adamnan, i, 11, 13 (Reeves). Montalembert, "Monks of the West," Vol. III, p. 76.

should be appointed under the national inspection, and that the monarch's own bard should be arch-poet and have superintendency over the rest.

Writing in 1720, Toland says: "The Irish have incomparably more ancient material for their history than either the English or the French, or any other European nation with whose manuscripts I have any acquaintance. In all conditions the Irish have been strangely solicitous, if not in some degree superstitious, about preserving their books and parchments, even those of them which are so as to be now partly un-intelligible.   Abundance through over-care have perished underground, the concealer not having skill for preserving them.[7]

"The most valuable pieces both in verse and prose were written by the Druidic ancestry; whereof some indeed have been interpolated after the prevailing of Christianity, which additions or alterations are, nevertheless, easily distinguished. And in these books were the rites and formularies of the Druids, together with their divinity and philosophy, especially their two grand doctrines of the eternity and incorrupti-bility of the universe.   Their laws were termed Celestial Judgments, and were only preserved in traditionary poems according to the institution of the Druids until committed to writing at the command of Conor Macnessa, King of Ulster, A.D. 48.

"The three greatest encouragers of learning among the early Irish monarchs were King Achaius, 1383 B.C., surnamed the Doctor of Ireland, who is

[7] "Libra Lintei," registers written on linen mentioned by Livy, 44 B.C.

said to have built at Tara an academy called the 'Court of the Learned.' It was he who ordained for every principal family hereditary antiquaries, or in case of incapacity, the most able of the same historical house, with ranks and privileges after the Druids.

"The next promoter of letters was King Tuathalius, first century A.D., who appointed a triennial revision of all the antiquaries' books by a committee of three kings or great lords, three Druids and three antiquaries. These were to cause whatever was approved and found valuable in those books to be transcribed into the Royal Book of Tara.[8]

"The third patron of literature was King Cormac, A.D. 266, who renewed the laws about the antiquaries, rebuilt and enlarged the academy at Tara for history, law and military training. He was an indefatigable distributor of justice, having written numerous laws still extant.[9]

"After the introduction of Christianity the Druid, where he accepted the new religion, became bishop or priest, but great numbers remained on the same footing, insomuch that for a long time after the English conquest the judges, bards, physicians and harpers held such tenures in Ireland.

"The O'Duvegans were hereditary bards; the O'Clerys and the O'Brodins were hereditary antiquaries; the O'Shiels and the O'Canvans were hereditary doctors; the Maglanchys were hereditary judges.

"The Druids did not at all times receive fair treat-

---

[8] Cusack, "Irish Nation," p. 33.
[9] Lady Ferguson, "The Irish Before the Conquest," p. 137.

ment from the Christians. Dudley Forbes, in a letter to an Irish writer, affirms that in St. Patrick's time no fewer than one hundred and eighty volumes relating to the affairs of the Druids were burnt in Ireland. What a deplorable extinction of arts and inventions; what an unspeakable detriment to learning. What a dishonour upon human understanding has the cowardly proceeding of the ignorant, or rather the interested at all times occasioned."[10]

Moore, the poet, when undertaking to write the history of Ireland, spoke slightingly of the value to the historian of Ireland, of the materials afforded by native manuscripts. In the year 1839, Moore, in company with Dr. Petrie, visited the Royal Irish Academy and was shown a number of ancient books useful for historical research and reference. Moore, on briefly scanning these books, turned to Dr. Petrie and said: "Petrie, these huge tomes could not have been written by fools or for any foolish purpose. I never knew anything about them before, and I had no right to have undertaken the 'History of Ireland'." And from that day Moore, it is said, lost all heart for going on with his "History of Ireland," and it was only the importunity of the publishers which induced him to bring out the remaining volume.[11]

The bards survived the merging of Druidism into Christianity for centuries and enjoyed their ancient honours and privileges in many places down to the reign of Queen Elizabeth. Until 1746 the bards of Munster continued to hold their half-yearly sessions in the County of Limerick.

[10] Toland, "Hist. of the Druids," pp. 82, 93.
[11] Matthew Arnold, "Celtic Literature," p. 44.

Like the bards, the judge survived the fall of the Druidical system. They had for successors and representatives those who in English are called Brehon (from the Celtic word "breathamh") which means "judge."

Cusack says that the whole system of government and legislation was patriarchal—indicative of an eastern origin; that in the Brehon laws—said to be the oldest code of laws in Europe—there are evidences which look very like a trace of Jewish tradition.[12]

Sir Henry Maine observed: "We who are able here to examine coolly the ancient Irish law in an authentic form can see that it is a very remarkable body of archaic law, unusually pure from its origin."[13]

[12] Cusack, "Irish Nation," pp. 99-103.
[13] "Early Hist. of Institutions," p. 19.

CHAPTER VII

ROMANS AND DRUIDISM

THE first decree against the Druids was enacted by the Emperor Tiberius,[1] under the plausible pretext of punishing them for offering human sacrifice, a decree as cruel as the pretext was false. The real reason was to destroy their influence in the state, an influence which extended through all the tribes.

"When the Romans," observed Cleland, "effected a footing in Britain they found in Druidism a constant and implacable enemy to their usurpation. They would have been glad to introduce their own religion, but to that point there was an invincible obstacle in the horror and contempt of the natives for a religion formed by a corruption of their own allegories which made the name of the Roman gods as familiar to them as Julius Cæsar states, but in a sense which excluded them from reception in a divine one."[2]

The report on the Druids as given by Suetonius Claudius, and passed on to posterity by other Roman historians, accusing them of arranging for frightful holocausts of victims in wicker cages has nothing but the assertion of this hostile Roman general to support it. The same historians accused the early Christians

[1] Toland, "Hist. of the Druids," p. 61, note.
[2] "Ancient Celtica," p. 13.

of "abominable practices."[3] The Romans did indeed, themselves, on many occasions burn the houses of the Britons which were, in the case of the poorer inhabitants, made of wicker-work covered with clay.

Bishop Browne describes the work of an antiquarian who dug up one of the dome-shaped hillocks and found the remains of the old British houses of wicker-work, the impress of the wicker remaining on the burnt clay, as indelible as the writing upon Assyrian monuments.[4] The Roman story is a palpable invention to cover their own inhuman methods of warfare.

The Druidic religion, like the Jewish and Christian, was diametrically opposed to the rest of the world. Druidism and Christianity were both marked for destruction by the Romans. Athenagoras, A.D. 176, in his work entitled "An Embassy," concerning the Christians, carefully describes and indignantly repudiates the three charges of atheism, cannibalism and lust, which were commonly urged against Christians in connection with their Eucharists, and pleads for an impartial trial that would lead to a just verdict.

In the case of Christianity all efforts to bring it into opprobrium and to annihilation were overcome. It lived to vindicate its quality and to cover the world with its beneficent institutions and influence.

With Druidism the case was different; at the very

---

[3] *Vide* Nero: "Those whom the vulgar call Christians are detested because of their scandalous practices."

[4] "The Christian Church in these Islands before the Coming of Augustine," p. 47.

beginning of the Christian era it quickly dissolved as a separate organisation. Druidism eagerly accepted a fuller revelation and became merged in Christianity. The immediate need, therefore, was not the defence of the principles and practice of the Druidic religion, of which hitherto very little had been perpetuated in writing. Consequently, real knowledge of its nature decayed, and ignorant or malevolent representations, false in their beginnings, continue, pitifully, to be accepted without investigation, as if they had come from the very source of Truth.

In A.D. 61 Suetonius Paulinus, the legate in Britain, proceeded to carry out instructions received from Rome to extirpate Druidism at any cost.[5] The Roman army, including the Ninth Legion from Lincoln, may be pictured moving along Watling Street, through Chester, where they were joined by the *vexillarii* and other auxiliary forces on their way to Anglesey, where great numbers of Druidic priests had taken refuge. The co-operation of the Second Augusta, stationed at Caerlleon-on-Usk, was refused by the præfectus—from motives of jealousy.[6]

Tacitus, patently unsympathetic with the gallant defenders of Britain, graphically describes the massacre of the priests which took place on that occasion. The Anglesey massacre had terrified the consciences of its perpetrators as it had roused to fury the passions of the whole population. The war from that moment became a religious war. Suetonius

[5] Tacitus, "Annals," XIV, ch. xxx.
[6] Tacitus. "Vita Agric.," 16.

was recalled. Tacitus assigns as the cause "The revolt of all Britain."[7] The Ninth Legion was completely broken at Anglesey; it afterwards received its full complement of men from Germany.[8]

The powerful resistance offered by the native tribes to the Roman invasions was mainly due to the exalted doctrine of the indestructibility of the soul taught by their religion.

Among the Celtic nations the person of the Druid was always sacred and inviolable; this was even the case with respect to the bard who was captured while encouraging his warriors in the midst of tribal conflict; the bards, while abhorring war themselves, and ever striving for peace, when conflict became inevitable accompanied their tribal or clan fighting men with words and songs of encouragement. The Romans, however, did not recognise the rule of inviolability; when they found the bard in the ranks of the enemy they consigned him to a worse fate than that of the rest of the captives.

The cumulative evidence of history is that Druidism and Christianity had no greater enemy than Imperial Rome. In striking contrast to Roman intolerance there is one feature of the religion of the ancient Britons spoken of with admiration by all writers—its freedom from intolerance. Druidism knew of no such violation of others' rights as persecution; there is no record of any missionary to Britain having suffered martyrdom under Druidism. It has been well said that among the Druids there were numerous

---

[7] Vita Agric., 5, 18.
[8] Tacitus, "Annals," XIV, ch. xxxviii.

confessors of Christianity, but no martyrs.[9]   The paganism of civilised Rome had its thousands of victims among the early Christians; the paganism, so-called, of Britain had none—and it would be well if the same could be said of some of the forms of Christianity which followed.

[9] Stukeley, "Stonehenge," p. 2.

CHAPTER VIII

DRUIDIC SURVIVALS

MEGALITHIC remains in Britain are uninscribed and unwrought; no graven image of any kind has been discovered of pre-Roman origin in Great Britain.

It is a remarkable circumstance that while statues of gods and goddesses prevail throughout the heathen sites of Egyptian, Greek, Roman and other idolatrous nations, not a vestige of an idol or image has ever been found in Britain.

The gigantic monoliths placed in circles and the piles of stones were alike unhewn. These piles were called si'uns or carns, and in the north of England known as laws or lows, placed usually on the summits of hills and mounds, and so disposed as to lie in sight of one of the other carns of the system. Many places in the British Isles are denominated from these carns or lows. The similarity of si'un with the Hebrew word "Zion," the Mount of Stone (as the name Zion means), is striking.

On May-eve, and on the first day of November, the Druids caused prodigious fires to be made on these si'uns or carns, which afforded a wonderful illumination over the whole country. Those on the first of May were to obtain a blessing on the fruits of the earth, that they might grow prosperously. Those on the first of November were a thanksgiving for finishing their harvest.

There are survivals in many parts of the Scottish Highlands of Druidic religious customs: places where the dead are borne sun-wise in their progress towards the place of sepulture. A boat going to sea must first go sun-wise. A man or woman immediately after marriage must take a turn sun-wise. Everything that is to move prosperously must, among many of the Celts, first move sun-wise.

Some of our great fairs may be traced to their origin in the days when our forefathers assembled on the fairfield close to the circle on the three great festivals of the year.[1] The name Mayfair, in London, is a survival from Druidic times, and where down to the Middle Ages great fairs were held. A large portion of downland half a mile from Stonehenge is still called the fairfield.

Close to many of the Druidic circles were places of assembly, called maidans (now maiden), and in most of the places where assembly and free speech are allowed to-day the custom and "right" of the people may be traced back to Druidic times.

Attached to the Druidic circles was the "sanctuary" or "place of refuge." When the London City Circle became merged in the Christian Church of St. Martin-le-Grand, where the General Post Office now stands, privilege of sanctuary survived there until the reign of James the First; and to this day the space fronting the west doors of Westminster Abbey is known as "Broad Sanctuary."

The Beltane or spring festival of Druidism became our Easter: the summer solstice or White-sun-tide

[1] R. H. Cunnington, "Stonehenge and its Date," p. 32.

became our Whitsuntide, and the mid-winter festival, when the mistletoe was gathered with gold sickles, became our Christmas.

So favourably impressed were some of our early reformers with the principles of Druidism that they embodied certain Druidic laws and ideas in their new codes; for instance, it is to St. Swithin, the first chancellor-bishop, the Church owes the revival and restoration by statute of the Druidic law of tithes. [2]

The Druidic triads are a heritage that should be valued for their simple beauty and the noble thoughts to which they give expression. Matthew Arnold says: "What a feeling for style in composition is manifested in the famous Welsh Triads. We may put aside all the vexed questions as to their greater or lesser antiquity, and still what important witness they bear to the genius for literary style of the people who produced them." [3]

According to Max Müller, these Triads are the oldest literature in the oldest living language in Europe; and again:

"If the study of Celtic languages and Celtic antiquities deserves to be encouraged anywhere it is surely in England . . . in order to supply sound material and guiding principles to the critical student of the ancient history and the ancient language of Britain, to excite an interest in what still remains of Celtic antiquities, whether in manuscript or in genuine stone monuments, and thus to preserve

---

[2] The original Charter is in the British Museum, written in the year 854.
[3] "Celtic Literature," p. 112.

F—c

such national heirlooms from neglect or utter destruction."[4]

A note to Lord Lytton's "King Arthur" says: "The Triads indeed are of various dates, but some bear the mark of a very remote antiquity, wholly distinct alike from the philosophy of the Romans and the mode of thought prevalent in the earlier ages of the Christian era; in short, anterior to all the recorded conquests of the Cymrian people. These, like proverbs, appear the wrecks and fragments of some primeval ethics or philosophical religion. Nor are such remarkable alone for the purity of the notions they inculcate relative to the Deity; they have often, upon matters less spiritual, the delicate observation, as well as the profound thought of reflective wisdom. Nor were the Druids of Britain inferior to those with whom the sages of the Western and Eastern worlds came into contact. On the contrary, even to the time of Caesar, the Druids of Britain excelled in science and repute those of Gaul, and to their schools the neophites were sent."

The spiritual character of Druidical teaching is illustrated in the following Triads:

"The three foundations of Druidism: Peace, Love, Justice.

"The three things God alone can do: endure the eternities of infinity; participate of all being without changing; renew everything without annihilating it.

"There are three Primeval Unities and more than one of each cannot exist: One God, one Truth, and one Point of Liberty where all opposites preponderate.

[4] "Selected Essays," Vol. I, p. 110.

"Three things proceed from the three Primeval Unities: all of Life; all that is Good; and all that is Power.

"The three primary principles of Wisdom: Wisdom to the laws of God; Concern for the welfare of mankind; Suffering with fortitude all the accidents of life.

"The three primary ornaments of Wisdom: Love; Truth; Courage.

"Three things that make a man equal to an angel: The love of every good; the love of exercising charity; the love of pleasing God.

"There are three men that all ought to look on with affection: he that with affection looks on the face of the earth; that is delighted with rational works of art; and that looks lovingly on little infants.

"Three duties of every man: Worship God; Be just to all men; Die for your country."

One of the leading maxims of the Druids was to examine without prejudice all matters that came under their observation.

The Druidical teaching concerning man's spiritual nature is comprised in the following Triad:

"In every person there is a soul.
In every soul there is intelligence.
In every intelligence there is thought.
In every thought there is either good or evil.
In every evil there is death.
In every good there is life.
In every life there is God."

A great deal of nonsense is spoken and believed

about the dragon, the emblem of Wales; many give it a religious significance, connecting it in some way with the devil; others with the monster with which St. George had dispute. It has no connection with either. In the ancient British language "dragon" was the name given to a leader in war:[5] the prefix "pen" or "head" was introduced to indicate the chief leader, and as the premier tribe or people of Britain the Welsh continue to display the flag on which is depicted the dragon.

The Welsh also hold the oldest religious symbolic emblem in these islands. This emblem, the leek, is as ancient as the Druidic Order itself, and is symbolic of the circles at which the inhabitants foregathered for worship.[6] The leek is still depicted on the badge of the Druidic Order of Wales.

To Wales belongs the most ancient religious emblem, the leek; and the most ancient secular or national emblem, the dragon.

Perhaps in the "three feathers" borne in the crest of the Prince of Wales, and in the Government mark known as the "broad arrow," we possess the most notable of any, and the most universally known survival from Druidic times. It is not so well known, however, that the "three feathers" and the "broad arrow" had their origin in the Druidic symbol for the ineffable name of the Deity. Three rays of light. Every Druid priest bore these in gold on the front of his tiara. A coin in the British Museum, inscribed

[5] Gibbon, "Decline and Fall of Roman Empire," Vol. V, p. 369. Gildas (p. 29) describes Maelgwn as "Island Dragon."
[6] Massey, "Book of Beginnings," Vol, I, p. 89.

CUNO (Cunobelinus 14 B.C.), representing a horse galloping to the left, displays as an accessory symbol a diadem with a plume of ostrich feathers.

Edward III adopted the symbol, the sign of spiritual and temporal power of the ancient Celtic kings and priests as the "cognisance" of his son, the Black Prince. In the form of three ostrich feathers the three golden rays have been borne from that time by successive Princes of Wales.

We find the broad arrow cut by the ordnance surveyors as a level mark, alike upon solitary mountain peak and kerbstone of crowded alley—the sacred symbol that proclaims from long ago and from generation to generation the national faith in the protecting power of the Almighty.

The motto of the Druids, "The truth against the world," survives to the present day as the motto of the Druidic Order of Wales.

The revived Druidic Gorsedd of Wales held each year at the Eisteddfod presents a picture of those vast assemblies at which the ancient Britons foregathered in the practice of their religion. The circle is formed of twelve unhewn stones; in the centre is the Maen Llog or Logan Stone, symbolic of the "House of God." Twelve bards, one by each stone, guard the circle to-day as in times past, and two keepers of the gate are stationed at the entrance on the east side.

The magnificent regalia of the Order is borne in the procession before the Archdruid, in which is included the sword surmounted by its crystal and emblematic dove. The Hirlas Horn, symbolic of authority, the drinking vessel of the ancient Druids, and used by them for sacramental purposes. It is possible that our custom of drinking healths may be traced to this ancient Druidic ritual.

The ceremonial invocation, said to be as old as the Druidic Order, is in the Welsh language, very impressive. Perhaps it suffers somewhat in the following English translation:

> "Grant, O God, Thy Protection,
> And in Protection, Strength,
> And in Strength, Understanding,
> And in Understanding, Knowledge,
> And in Knowledge, the Knowledge of Justice,
> And in the Knowledge of Justice, the Love of it,
> And in that Love, the Love of all Existences,
> And in the Love of all Existences, the love of God.
> God and all Goodness."

At the moment of prayer all the bards bow the head toward the Maen Llog or centre stone. In the survival of this simple ceremony is preserved a picture of the solemn assemblies of our forefathers and a very inspiring link with the past.

> "Within the stones of federation there
> On the green turf, and under the blue sky,
> A noble band—the bards of Britain stood,
> "Their heads in rev'rence bow'd and bare of foot,
> A deathless brotherhood."
>
> *Southey*, "Madoc."

CHAPTER IX

THE CULDEES

To TRACE the history of the Culdees from the days of
St. Columba is a comparatively easy task; to find
their origin is more difficult. On the minute examina-
tion which such an investigation involves the name
Culdee is discovered to have quite a different origin
from that usually assigned to it.

The obscurity of the origin of the Culdich
(Anglicised Culdees) has led many writers to assume
that their name was derived from their life and work.
The interpretations "Cultores Dei" (Worshippers of
God) and "Gille De" (Servants of God) are ingenious
but do not go far to solve the problem. Culdich is
still in use among some of the Gael. Of "Cultores
Dei" and "Gille de" they know nothing.[1]

John Colgan, the celebrated hagiologist and
topographer, translates Culdich "*quidam advanae*"—
certain strangers[2]—particularly strangers from a
distance; this would seem an unaccountable interpre-
tation of the name for these early Christians were it
not for the statement of Freculphus[3] that certain
friends and disciples of Our Lord, in the persecution
that followed His Ascension, found refuge in Britain

---

[1] Rev. T. McLauchlan, "The Early Scottish Church," p. 431.
[2] "Trias Thaumaturga," p. 156.b.
[3] Freculphus, apud Godwin, p. 10. See Cave, "Hist. Lit.", ii, 18.

in A.D. 37.[4] Further, there is the strong unvarying tradition in the west of England of the arrival in this country in the early days A.D. of certain "Judean refugees." It seems impossible to avoid the conclusion that Colgan's Culdich, "certain strangers," were one and the same with these refugees who found asylum in Britain; who were hospitably received by Arviragus (Caractacus) king of the West Britons or Silures and temporarily settled at a Druidic College. Land to the extent of twelve hides, or ploughs, on which they built the first Christian Church, was made over to them in free gift by Arviragus. This land has never been taxed. Of the twelve ploughs of land conferred by Arviragus on this Church, the Domesday Survey, A.D. 1088, supplies confirmation. "The Domus Dei, in the great monastery of Glastingbury. This Glastingbury Church possesses in its own villa XII hides of land which have never paid tax."[5]

These "strangers" who brought the Christian Faith to these islands continued to be known to the inhabitants of Britain as the Culdich (Culdees). The name adhered to the converted Druid priests and their successors in the British Church, founded on Apostolic lines, by these first heralds of the Gospel.[6] Eastern usages continued in this Church for centuries.[7]

Writers who have made enquiry into the history

[4] Baronius ad. ann. 306. Vatican MSS. Nova Legenda Anglia, Vol. II, p. 78. Iolo MSS. Bouche, "Defense de la Foi de Provence pour ses Saints."

[5] Domesday Survey, fol., p. 449.

[6] See M'Callum, "Hist. of Culdees," p. 19.

[7] F. E. Warren, "Liturgy and Ritual of the Celtic Church," p. 55. See Mylnes, "Hist. of the Bishops of Dunkeld."

of the Culdees, while failing to discover the origin of the name, agree that it was the name by which Christianised Druids in Britain were known before a century had passed.

In Spelman's "Concilia" is an engraving of a brass plate which was formerly affixed to a column erected to mark the exact site of the church at Glastonbury. "The first ground of God, the first ground of the Saints in Britain, the rise and foundation of all religion in Britain, the burial place of the Saints." [8] This plate was dug up at Glastonbury and came into Spelman's possession.

From a "mass of evidences" to which William of Malmesbury gave careful study, the antiquity of the Church of Glastonbury was unquestionable. He says, "from its antiquity called, by way of distinction, 'Ealde Chirche,' that is the Old Church, of wattle-work at first, savoured somewhat of heavenly sanctity, even from its very foundation, and exhaled it all over the country, claiming superior reverence though the structure was mean. Hence, here arrived whole tribes of the lower orders, thronging every path; hence assembled the opulent, divested of their pomp; hence it became the crowded residence of the religious and the literary. For, as we have heard from men of elder time, here Gildas, an historian neither unlearned nor inelegant, captivated by the sanctity of the place, took up his abode for a series of years. This Church, then, is certainly the oldest I am acquainted with in England and from this circumstance derives its name. . . . Moreover there are

[8] "Concilia," Vol. I, p. 9. Epistolae ad Gregorium Papam.

documents of no small credit, which have been
discovered in certain places, to the following effect:
'No other hands than those of the disciples of Christ
erected the Church of Glastonbury' . . . for if
Philip the Apostle preached to the Gauls, as
Freculfus relates in the fourth chapter of his second
book, it may be believed that he also planted the
Word on the hither side of the channel."[9]

Further support for the early introduction of
Christianity to Britain is gathered from the following
widely diverse sources:

Eusebius of Cæsarea speaks of apostolic missions
to Britain as matters of notoriety: "The Apostles
passed beyond the ocean to the isles called the
Britannic Isles."[10]

Gildas, the British historian, writing in A.D. 542,
says: "We certainly know that Christ, the True Son,
afforded His light, the knowledge of His precepts, to
our Island in the last year of the reign of Tiberius
Caesar, A.D. 37."[11]

Sir Henry Spelman, in his "Concilia," states:
"We have abundant evidence that this Britain of ours
received the Faith, and that from the disciples of
Christ Himself, soon after the Crucifixion;"[12] and
Polydore Vergil observes that Britain was of all
kingdoms the first that received the Gospel.[13]

Tertullian of Carthage, A.D. 208, the embodiment
of the highest learning of that age, tells us that the

[9] Malmes., "Hist. of the Kings," pp. 19, 20.
[10] "De Demonstratione Evangelii," Lib. III.
[11] "De Excidio Britanniae," Sect. 8, p. 25.
[12] "Concilia," fol., p. 1.
[13] Lib. II.

Christian Church in the second century extended to "all the boundaries of Spain, and the different nations of Gaul and parts of Britain inaccessible to the Romans but subject to Christ."[14]

Origen, in the third century, states: "The power of Our Lord is with those who in Britain are separated from our coasts."[15]

"From India to Britain," writes St. Jerome, A.D. 378, "all nations resound with the death and resurrection of Christ."[16]

Arnobius, A.D. 400, on the same subject, writes: "So swiftly runs the word of God that within the space of a few years, His word is concealed neither from the Indians in the East nor from the Britons in the West."[17]

Chrysostom, Patriarch of Constantinople, A.D. 402, supplies evidence in these words: "The British Isles, which are beyond the sea, and which lie in the ocean, have received the virtue of the Word. Churches are there found and altars erected. Though thou shouldst go to the ocean, to the British Isles, there thou shouldst hear all men everywhere discoursing matters out of the Scriptures."[18]

The cumulative evidence of early historians leaves no shadow of doubt that Britain was one of the first, if not the first, country to receive the Gospel, and that the apostolic missionaries were instrumental

[14] "Adv. Judaeos," ch. vii. Def. Fidei, p. 179.
[15] Origen, "Hom. VI in Lucae."
[16] "Hom. in Isaim," ch. liv, and Epist. xiii ad Paulinum.
[17] "Ad Psalm," cxlviii.
[18] Chrysostomi, "Orat o Theo Xristos."

in influencing the change whereby the native religion of Druidism merged into Christianity.[19]

"Our forefathers, you will bear in mind, were not generally converted, as many would fain represent, by Roman missionaries. The heralds of salvation who planted Christianity in most parts of England were trained in British schools of theology and were firmly attached to those national usages which had descended to them from the most venerable antiquity."[20]

The first converts of the Culdees were Druids: the Druids of Britain, in embracing Christianity, found no difficulty in reconciling the teaching of the Culdees, or "Judean refugees" with their own teaching of the resurrection and the immortality of the soul.

From "Ecclesiastical Antiquities of the Cymry" we learn that the Silurian Druids embraced Christianity on its first promulgation in these islands, and that in right of their office they were exclusively elected as Christian ministers, though their claims to national privileges as such were not finally sanctioned until the reign of Lles ab Coel (Lucius), A.D. 156. All the Bardic privileges and immunities were recognised by law until the reign of this king.

"And those Druids that formerly had dominion of the Britons' Faith become now to be helpers of their joy, and are become the leaders of the blind, which through God's mercy hath continued in this Island

---

[19] Holinshed, "Chronicles," p. 23.
[20] Soames, "Bampton Lectures," pp. 112, 257.

ever since through many storms and dark mists of time until the present day."[21]

This Christian king (Lucius), the third in descent from Caradoc, and grandson of Pudens and Claudia,[22] built the first minster on the site of a Druidic Cor or Circle at Winchester, and at a National Council held there in A.D. 156, established Christianity the national religion as the natural successor to Druidism; when the Christian ministry was inducted into all the rights of the Druidic hierarchy, tithes included.[23] The change over from Druidism was not a mere arbitrary act of the king, for, according to the Druidic law there were three things that required the unanimous vote of the nation: Deposition of the Sovereign; Suspension of law; Introduction of novelties in religion.[24]

Archbishop Ussher quotes twenty-three authors, including Bede and Nennius, on this point, and also brings in proof from ancient British coinage.[25] So uncontested was the point, that at the Council of Constance it was pleaded as an argument for British precedence.

The fact that Lucius established Christianity as the state religion excludes the claim of the Latin Church to that eminence. That this early establishment was acknowledged beyond the confines of Britain is well expressed by Sabellius, A.D. 250: "Christianity was

[21] Nath. Bacon, "Laws and Govt. of England," p. 3.

[22] Moncaeus Atrebas, "In Syntagma," p. 38.

[23] Nennius (ed. Giles), p. 164. Book of Llandâv., pp. 26, 68, 289. MS. in Bibliothecâ Cottonianâ. Triad 35.

[24] Morgan's "British Cymry."

[25] Ussher (Ed. 1639), pp. 5, 7, 20.

privately confessed elsewhere, but the first nation
that proclaimed it as their religion, and called itself
Christian, after the name of Christ, was Britain,"[26]
and Genebrard remarks: "The glory of Britain
consists not only in this, that she was the first country
which in a national capacity publicly professed
herself Christian, but that she made this confession
when the Roman Empire itself was pagan and a
cruel persecutor of Christianity."

The writer of "Vale Royal" states: "The Christian
faith and baptism came into Chester in the reign of
Lucius, king of the Britons, probably from Cambria,
about A.D. 140."[27]

For over one hundred years before the reign of this
king, Christianity had been taught and preached in
Britain.

A Welsh Triad mentions Amesbury (Avebury), in
Wiltshire, as one of the three great Druidic "Cors"
or colleges of Britain, and one of the earliest to be
converted to Christian uses. In the church attached
to this college there were two thousand four hundred
"saints," that is, there were a hundred for every hour
of the day and night in rotation, perpetuating the
praise of God without intermission. This mode of
worship was very usual in the early Church.[28]

Missionaries are said to have come over from
Glastonbury, only thirty miles distant, to instruct the
Druids of Amesbury in the Christian faith. When the
Druids adopted and preached Christianity, their

---

[26] Sabell. Enno, Lib. VII, ch. v.
[27] King's "Vale Royal," Bk. II, p. 25.
[28] Baronius ad. Ann. 459 ex Actis Marcelli.

universities were turned into Christian colleges and the Druid priests became Christian ministers: the transition was, to them, a natural one.

Numerous writers have commented on the remarkable coincidence which exists between the two systems—Druidism and Christianity. Amongst the Druidic names for the Supreme God which they had in use before the introduction of Christianity were the terms: "Distributor," "Governor," "The Mysterious One," "The Wonderful," "The Ancient of Days," terms distinctly of Old Testament origin.[29]

Taliesen, a bard of the sixth century, declares: "Christ, the Word from the beginning, was from the beginning our Teacher, and we never lost His teaching. Christianity was a new thing in Asia, but there never was a time when the Druids of Britain held not its doctrines."[30]

In the days of Giraldus Cambrensis (twelfth century), as a result of Roman Catholic doctrine, martyrdom and celibacy were much over-rated, and it was thought a reproach to the Druids that none of their saints had "cemented" the foundation of the Church with their blood, all of them being confessors, and not one gaining the crown of martyrdom.[31] An absurd charge, blaming the people for their reasonableness, moderation and humanity, and taxing the new converts for not provoking persecution in order to gain martyrdom.

It is not contended that every individual Druid and

[29] G. Smith, "Religion of Anc. Britain," ch. ii, p. 37.
[30] Morgan, "St. Paul in Britain," p. 73.
[31] Topograph. Hibern. Distinct. III, cap xxix.

Bard accepted Christianity on its first promulgation in Britain; even after Christianity had become the national religion, petty kings, princes and the nobility retained, in many instances, Druids and Bards. Druidism did not entirely cease until nearly a thousand years after Christ.

Had the large collection of British archives and MSS. deposited at Verulam as late as A.D. 860 descended to our time, invaluable light would have been thrown on this as on many other subjects of native interest. [32]

Toland states that two Druids acted as tutors to the two daughters of Laegaire (Leary) the high king of Ireland, in whose reign St. Patrick conducted his great revival; that Ida and Ono, Lords of Roscommon, were Druids and that Ono presented his fortress of Imleach-Ono to St. Patrick, who converted it into the religious house of Elphin, later an episcopal see. [33]

We read in an historical essay, "The Ancient British Church," by the Rev. John Pryce, which was awarded the prize at the National Eisteddfod of 1876, these words: "In this distant corner of the earth (Britain) cut off from the rest of the world, unfrequented except by merchants from the opposite coast of Gaul, a people who only conveyed to the Roman mind the idea of untamed fierceness, was being prepared for the Lord.

"Forecasting the whole from the beginning and at

[32] *Vide* Matthew of Westminster.   William of Malmesbury. Life of Eadmer.
[33] Toland, "Hist. of the Druids," pp. 68, 91.

length bringing the work to a head, the Divine Logos unveiled Himself to them in the person of Christ, as the realisation of their searching instincts and the fulfilment of their highest hopes. It would be difficult to conceive of Christianity being preached to any people for the first time under more favourable conditions. There was hardly a feature in their national character in which it would not find a chord answering and vibrating to its touch.

"Theirs was not the sceptical mind of the Greek, nor the worn-out civilisation of the Roman, which even Christianity failed to quicken into life, but a religious impulsive imagination—children in feeling and knowledge, and therefore meet recipients of the good news of the kingdom of heaven.

"To a people whose sense of future existence was so absorbing that its presentiment was almost too deeply felt by them, the preaching of Jesus and the Resurrection would appeal with irresistible force. There was no violent divorce between the new teaching and that of their own Druids, nor were they called upon so much to reverse their ancient faith as to lay it down for a fuller and more perfect revelation."

Well has the Swedish poet, Tegner, in "Frithiofs Saga," pictured the Norse glimmerings of the dawn of Gospel day, when he describes the old priest as prophesying:

> "All hail, ye generations yet unborn!
> Than us far happier; ye shall one day drink
> That cup of consolation, and behold

The torch of Truth illuminate the world.
Yet do not us despise; for we have sought
With earnest zeal and unaverted eye,
To catch one ray of that ethereal light.
Alfader still is one, and still the same;
But many are his messengers divine."

CHAPTER X

THE EARLY BRITISH CHURCH

THE name by which the British Church was first known in these islands was the Culdee Church, the natural result of Christianity having been introduced by the Culdich or "refugees." The ecclesiastics of this Church, composed chiefly of Christianised Druids, became known as the Culdees, and not until the Latin aggression, five centuries later, were they referred to as the British clergy, in contra-distinction to the clergy of the Roman Church. The fact is well established from the testimony of early writers and councils that, through the Culdee Church, the, National Church of Britain is the Mother Church of Christendom.

The Culdees established Christian churches, monasteries and colleges, chiefly in remote places, where they fled from persecution by the Romans. Enlii (i.e. Bardsey), off the coast of Wales, once afforded shelter to twenty thousand Christians. Lindisfarne, Iona and many of the islands off the west coast of Scotland, and inaccessible parts of Ireland, were all inhabited in the early days of Christianity by the Culdees.

Eurgan, daughter of Caradoc, and wife of Salog, Prince of old Sarum, founded a college of twelve Christian Druids (Culdee initiates) at Caer Urgan,[1]

[1] Iolo MSS., p. 343.

or Llantwit Major. This college must therefore have been established in the first century, as Caradoc flourished A.D. 60.

The Culdee Church was ruled by bishops[2] and elders—elder and priest (from presbyteros) being synonymous terms.[3] From an ancient authority we learn that the Culdees made no alteration in the terms used by the Druids; they also retained the white dress of the Druidic priests.[4] A superintendent among the Druids in Britain was a deon, i.e. a dean.

The clergy of the early Church came into office hereditarily; the principle of hereditary succession ran through the whole Celtic polity. The crown was hereditary with certain modifications peculiar to the Celts themselves. The bards were hereditary without much reference to qualification. In Ireland there was a hereditary succession in the bishopric of Armagh for fifteen generations.

Giraldus Cambrensis, Bishop of St. Davids, in the twelfth century, a strong supporter of the Latin Church, complains of the Culdee Church, that "the sons, after the deaths of their fathers, succeed to the ecclesiastical benefices, not by election, but by hereditary right."[5]

Monasteries, or more correctly, colleges, were attached to the early British churches.[6] Seats of

[2] Tertullian terms Bishops "Presidents." "De Corona" Milit. iii. 4. (A.D. 211.)
[3] Cyprian in Ep. i, 1, applies the term Levite to a Presbyter. (A.D. 230.)
[4] M'Callum, "Hist. of Culdees," pp. 158, 159.
[5] Book of Llandâv, p. 279. "Topograph. Hibern. Distinct," III, cap xxix.
[6] Dugdale, "Monasticon," Vol. I, p. 2. D. M'Callum, "Hist. of Culdees," p. 159.

learning were styled Cathair Culdich—the Chair of
the Culdees. [7] The mode of life in these monasteries
was, however, very different from that of the
generality of those institutions that have been called
monasteries in later ages. In each college there were
twelve brethren, and one who was "provost" or
"abbot"; wherever the Culdees formed a new settlement or college of presbyters, the fixed number of the
council was twelve, following the example of the
Apostles of Jesus Christ.

Gildas states that in old phraseology—*sanctorum
speluncae*—the monasteries, were the caves of the
saints; [8] this makes intelligible the old records of the
Culdees that they lived in kels or caves in Britain.
Kings and the nobility frequently passed their last
years in the peace and seclusion of these monasteries.

According to Jamieson, there is a general tradition
in the Highlands of Scotland that the Culdees
immediately succeeded the Druids as the ministers
of religion. [9] The tradition is supported by a circumstance of an interesting nature, which has been
mentioned by several writers, that "clachan," the
name still given in the Highlands to the place where
a church stands, belonged originally to a Druidical
temple. Hence it is still said: "Will you go to the
stones?" or "Have you been to the stones?"; that is,
"Will you go to," or "Have you been to church?"
At the end of the seventeenth century, in a Highland
parish of Scotland, an old man, who, although very

[7] Jamieson, "Hist. of Culdees," p. 35, note.
[8] De Ex. Brit., cc. xxxiii-xxxvi.
[9] James Macpherson, "Fingal" (Dissertation), p. 7. M'Callum,
"Hist. of Culdees," pp. 158, 159.

regular in his devotions, never addressed the Supreme Being by any other title than that of "Archdruid," accounting every other derogatory to the Divine Majesty.[10]

Adamnan, the successor and biographer of St. Columba, states that Columba was wont to say of the Lord Jesus: "Christ the Son of God is my Druid."[11]

Every fragment of such evidence is valuable, inasmuch as it manifests the true character of the Druids, and indicates the esteem in which even their memory was held long after Druidism had ceased as the national religion and had become merged in Christianity.

Archdeacon Monro, who made a tour of the Western Isles in 1549, begins his narrative with the Isle of Man, "which sometime, as old historiographers say, was wont to be the seat first ordained by Fynan, king of Scotland, to the priests and the philosophers, called in Latin 'Druids,' in English 'Culdees,' which were the first teachers of religion in Albion."[12]

The Culdees flourished increasingly from the first to the seventh century; kings and rulers of provinces united in enriching the Church.

Sir James Dalrymple observes that the common practice of the Culdees was to dedicate their principal churches to the Trinity, and not to the Virgin or any

[10] Jamieson's "Culdees," p. 25.

[11] Reeves "Life of Columba," p. 74. Petrie, "Tara Hill," pp. 205, 208.

[12] "Miscellanea Scotica," Vol. II, p. 133.

saint.[13] Sometimes, however, churches were named after their living founders.[14]

The early Christian missionaries did not seek a "diseart" or place of retirement, until their labours as active missionaries had come to an end; withdrawal from the world was not encouraged, as is evidenced by the words of a second century writer. "We are not Indian Brahmans or Gymnosophists who dwell in woods and exile themselves from ordinary human life; we sojourn with you in the world."

Writing of the early Church, Thomas Fuller (1608-1661) says: "Most of these men seem born under a travelling planet, seldom having their education in the place of their nativity; oft times composed of Irish infancy, British breeding and French preferment; taking a cowl in one country, a crozier in another, and a grave in a third. Neither bred where born, nor beneficed where bred, nor buried where beneficed, but wandering in several kingdoms."[15] In all probability it was this mode of training and life work which gave rise to the supposition in later years that there were three Saints Patrick, mention having been made of him in connection with Auvergne, Ireland and Nola.

Surprise is sometimes expressed that there are so few records of the Early British Church. The savage edicts of Roman emperors were directed not alone to the destruction of individuals who confessed the

---

[13] "Historic Collections," p. 248.
[14] F. E. Warren, "Liturgy and Ritual of the Celtic Church," p. 55.
[15] "Ch. Hist. of Britain," p. 121.

Christian Faith, but also to the destruction of the literature and records of the Church.

There were ten "high power" persecutions of the Christians under these tyrants, extending from A.D. 66 to A.D. 303; the last being that of Diocletian, which began in A.D. 290.[16] Bede says: "The Diocletian persecution was carried out incessantly for ten years, with burning of churches, outlawing of innocent persons and the slaughter of martyrs. At length it reached Britain in the year 300, and many persons with the constancy of martyrs died in the confession of the Faith." The records of the Church had now to be written, not with pen and ink, but in blood and flames of martyrdom. In the Edict of Diocletian, the Scriptures were to be carried away or destroyed, being regarded as books of magic; in this he was following older methods of suppression.

The British Church at this time lost the following by martyrdom: Amphibalus, Bishop of Llandaff; Alban of Verulam; Aaron and Julian, citizens and presbyters of Chester; Socrates, Bishop of York; Stephen, Bishop of London; Augulius, his successor; Nicholas, Bishop of Penrhyn (Glasgow); Melior, Bishop of Carlisle, and above ten thousand communicants in different grades of society.[17]

After the Diocletian persecutions had died out, the churches in Britain were again rebuilt,[18] and Christianity flourished to so great an extent that at

[16] Tillemont, Vol. IV, pp. 508 ff. Allard, "La Persecution de Diocletian," pp. 40, 41.
[17] Haddan & Stubbs, Vol. I, p. 32. Zozomen, "Hist. Eccles.," Vol. I, p. 6. Fuller, "Ch. Hist. of Britain," Vol. I, p. 40.
[18] Gildas, "De Exc. Brit.," Sec. 10, p.10.

the Council of Arles, in A.D. 314, the British Church was represented by three bishops and a presbyter, and again, at the Council of Sardica and Ariminium in the fourth century. It is interesting to notice that the three bishops who represented the British Church at the Council of Arles came from London, York and Caerlleon-on-Usk,[19] the former seats of the three Archdruids of Britain.

Against the British Church no charge of heretical doctrine has at any time been made, though the very prince of heretics, Pelagius, was one of its most prominent and learned Abbots.

The Pelagian heresy originated by Morien,[20] better known by his Latin name, Pelagius, twentieth Abbot of Bangor-on-Dee, Flintshire, was nothing more than an attempted revival of Druidism, and of the old Druidic ideas with regard to the nature and free will of man. The beauty of the Latin compositions of Pelagius, his extensive learning and reproachless life, facilitated the spread of the heresy everywhere; it was quickly suppressed in Britain.[21]

St. Hilary of Poictiers, in the latter part of the fourth century, wrote to the British Church: "I congratulate you upon having remained undefiled in the Lord, and untainted by all the contagion of detestable heresy. Oh, the unshaken steadfastness of your glorious conscience! Oh, house, firm on the

[19] Mansi Conciliorum Nova et ampliss. Collectio ii, p. 476. (New ed.) Eusebius on Socrates, v, 23. Concilia Compiled (1) J. Crabbe, (2) Labbé.

[20] Iolo MSS., pp. 42, 43.

[21] Rev. R. W. Morgan, "St. Paul in Britain," p. 161.

foundation of the faithful rock! Oh, the constancy of your uncontaminated will."[22]

During the storm which the Pelagian heresy caused in Britain, one of the greatest lights of the Culdee Church, St. Patrick, was, in the providence of God, being prepared for his great work of revivalist among the Irish people, Christianity, according to Gildas, having been planted in Ireland before the defeat of Queen Boudicca, A.D. 61.

Maelwyn or Patrick, the Apostle of Ireland, and of the Isle of Man, born at Llantwit Major, Glamorganshire,[23] A.D. 363, from whence he was taken prisoner and carried to Ireland, is by tradition a Culdee, and the son-in-law of a Bard;[24] by his own statement, the son of a presbyter[25] and grandson of a deacon, both of the British Church, St. Ilytds,[26] Llantwit Major, to which was attached a college.

Patrick's father, Calpurnius (not Patrick himself, as frequently erroneously stated) would appear to have been principal of this college, acting at the same time as an official of the Roman Empire, probably as broveratius (from broguiredd-a-twos), "district justiciary and chief." Patrick would in such case have early opportunity of acquiring a knowledge of Roman law and of British Church government.

Niall of the Nine Hostages, so-called because five provinces in Ireland and four in Scotia delivered

---

[22] Hilar. Pictav., "De Synodis."

[23] See Fryer's "Lantwit Major."

[24] Tirechan's "St. Patrick." (MS. in British Museum.) Egerton 93, fol. 13, ba.

[25] Styled "Presbyter" in "Book of Durrow," vit Reeve's Ed., p. 242.

[26] Cottonian MSS. Vespasian A, XIV. Printed in Rees' "Cambro British Saints."

hostages to him, changed the name of North Britain from Albania to Scotia at the request of a colony of the Dalriada, the Irish colonists who had been led by Fergus from Antrim to Argyllshire. Niall, in one of his raids, took Patrick prisoner from Llantwit Major to Ireland in A.D. 379. The captive escaped to Gaul, returning to Ireland nearly fifty years later as a missionary.

St. Patrick is said to have introduced the use of the Latin language,[27] the previous missionaries having used chiefly Greek.[28] Latin did not, however, rapidly supplant Greek. Professor H. Zimmer says: "It is almost a truism to say that whoever knew Greek on the Continent in the days of Charles the Bald (tenth century) was an Irishman or was taught by an Irishman."[29]

Bede does not mention Patrick for the very obvious reason that the Culdee hierarchy with its hereditary succession was obnoxious to Bede as an earnest adherent of the novel papal Church introduced in A.D. 664, but he speaks of his contemporary, Palladius,[30] and again for the very obvious reason that Palladius, a Caledonian and a Culdee, became, like Ninian,[31] an emissary of the Roman See, which was now resolutely setting itself to grasp the sceptre of universal dominion in the Christian Church.

Many of the saints of the British Church were at a

[27] Schöll, "De Eccles. Brit. Scotor. Hist. Fontibus," p. 17. Haddan & Stubbs "Councils," Vol. I, pp. 175, note. Tripartite Life of St. Patrick.

[28] Reeves, "Adamnan," p. 354.

[29] "Celtic Church in Britain and Ireland," p. 92.

[30] Eccles. Hist. ch. xiii.

[31] Ailred "Vit. Nin.," cap. ii. Bede, iii, 4, 5.

later date claimed by the Latin Church, and legends undeserving of the slightest credence grew around their names. Those who owed nothing to Rome in connection with their conversion, and who long struggled against her pretensions, were later claimed by the Latin Church as if they had been her most devoted adherents. This is especially noticeable in the case of St. Patrick, whose conversion was the result of early training in a British Christian home, who was all his life a Culdee, yet is now given the greatest prominence in Roman Catholic hagiology.

The great St. Columba, fourth in descent from Niall of the Nine Hostages, born A.D. 522, about fifty years after the death of St. Patrick, was associated with the Culdee Church of Iona for thirty-two years, where he arrived from Ireland, on Pentecost Eve in the year 565, with his twelve disciples. We are here given another instance of the faithfulness of the Culdees to first foundations in the formation of a new settlement.

There is a curious story told in connection with the landing of this little band. The island, Inis-nan-Druidneach (Isle of Druids), the native name for Iona, was the abode of Druids, whose predecessors had fled there from Roman Imperial persecution.[32] When St. Columba arrived, Adonellus tells us, he was opposed by these Druids, who disguised themselves in the habits of monks and pretended they had come to that place to preach the Gospel, and requested that he and his followers might betake

[32] Encyc. Brit. (eleventh ed.), Vol. XIV, p. 727. Llwyd, "Isle of Mona," p. 49.

themselves to some other place.[33] From this story, though somewhat distorted by the medieval historian, it is easily perceived that the Druids of Iona were already Christian, and were themselves teachers of the Gospel, and advised St. Columba to form a settlement elsewhere. That eventually St. Columba and his disciples settled down with these Druids is a matter of history. They built a monastery for their own accommodation, and then with his missionary disciples St. Columba turned his attention to Scotland, where Culdee missionaries had already taken the Gospel.

Of St. Columba, his friends tell of him that "he was angelical in look, brilliant in speech, holy in work, clear in intellect and just in council."

St. Columba did not recommend lengthened fasts (any more than long faces), but would have the brethren eat every day, that they might be able to work and pray every day.

One of his disciples and successors, Baithen, was distinguished not only for his holy life, but for his learning. "Know," said a learned man of his time,[34] "that there is no one on this side of the Alps, who is equal to him in knowledge of the Scriptures, and in the greatness of his learning. I do not compare the disciple with his master. Columba is not to be compared with philosophers and learned men, but with patriarchs and apostles."[35]

Surrounded by the stormy Atlantic, a more

---

[33] Adonellus, ii, 11.

[34] Fintan.

[35] Montalembert, "Monks of the West," Vol. III, p. 93.

desolate abode could hardly be imagined than Iona, and were it not for the ruins of the monastery, and the graves of the Norse kings around it, the traveller would never guess that it had been the resort of princes from distant lands, and had once echoed to the sound of prayers, psalms and anthems. For two hundred years Iona was the lighthouse for the western nations, whence missionaries went forth in all directions.

It is known that in Iona, in very ancient times, a great collection of books was made, and it is an interesting fact of history that Fergus II of Scotland, who in his youth assisted Alaric the Goth at the sack of Rome, A.D. 410, brought away, as part of the plunder, some valuable "geir," and a chest of books which he afterwards presented to the monastery of Iona, then known as Inis-nan-Druidneach (Isle of Druids). This presentation was made 164 years before St. Columba's date—clear evidence that St. Columba's famous library was founded by the Druids.

Eneas Silvius, afterwards Pope Pius II, sent a legate to Scotland to ascertain if the lost books of Titus Livy should be found among them. At a later date (1525) Master John Campbell, Treasurer to the King, found five old books which then consisted of nothing but broken leaves and very difficult to read. Boece says that "the reading sounded more like the eloquence of Salustius than of Livy."[36]

Fergus II is not to be confused with Fergus MacEarc, sixth century, who with his followers from

---

[36] Boece, "Scotorum Historiae," ed. J. Bellenden, 1531, p. 252.

Ireland settled in Caledonia. Fergus II (grandson of Ethodius, who was banished from Scotland and received by the King of Denmark) succeeded in recovering his birthright possessions and the crown of Scotland.[37]

[37] *Ibid.*

CHAPTER XI

THE ANGLO-SAXON INVASION

THE Anglo-Saxon invasion, actually of all the tribal settlements in Britain the most important and complete, took place between A.D. 446 and 501.

In these incursions the Jutes and Angles were the first to arrive; the Angles being, numerically, the strongest constituent, gave their name, in this country, to the entire group which on the Continent were known as Saxons.

Curiously enough a belief persists that the Anglo-Saxons on their first arrival in this country were entirely pagan, and that their conception of the Deity was expressed in the worship of numerous gods of their own imaginative creation: the exponents of this belief urge in support of it that memorials of these gods still exist, as, for instance, in the names of the days of the week: they cite Odin, in connection with Wednesday, as an outstanding example. Belief supported on such ground does not at all hold a position that is incontestable. Grimm says: "Among old Saxon, and all Teutonic nations, Odin signifies "Divinity"; Peterson likewise: "Odin's name bears allusion to mind or thought, and breathing; it is the quickening, creating Power; it denotes the all-pervading spiritual Godhead."[1]   Odin was, there-

[1] Oxford Icelandic Dictionary.

fore, the Scandinavian name for the Infinite Being, the central object of Christian worship to-day.[2]

Confusion on this point arose in the minds of historians, owing, perhaps, to the fact that Sigge, son of Fridulph, a pontiff prince of Azoff in the Crimea, 72 B.C., took the name of Odin[3] when he assumed the leadership of the early Saxons spiritually as well as temporally, and led them with magnetic instinct from Asgard to north-western Europe. As the Gisla-Saga says: "Sometimes a chief's name referred to the god he especially worshipped."[4]

Snorre, in his "Heimskringla" or Home Chronicles, tells how Odin was a heroic prince in the Black Sea region, with twelve peers and a great people straitened for room and how he led them across Europe. Odin and his peers became heroes to the descendants of these early Saxons and as such passed into legend and song.[5]

The modern Germans claim a share in the legends and traditions that have accumulated around the name of Odin; that illustrious individual, however, belonged exclusively to the Sakian (Saxon) race, and was in no way connected, ethnically, with the Germans.[6]

With the Anglo-Saxons, as with the Britons, the king was the last resort of justice and the source of honour and mercy; he was to be prayed for and

[2] *See* "Prelim. Dissert." Laing's "Heimskringla," p. 86.
[3] *See* H. Munro Chadwick, "The Origin of the English," p. 321.
[4] Oxford Icelandic Dictionary.
[5] Rollaston, "Mazzaroth," iii, 23.
[6] Bruce Hannay, "European and Other Race Origins," p. 456.

revered of all men of their own will without command, and was the especial protector of all churches, of widows and of foreigners. [7]

The Anglo-Saxon invasions had the effect of gradually pushing the Celts to the west of England and south-west Scotland. When this occurred and the Archbishops of Caerleon-on-Usk, London and York saw all the churches in their jurisdiction lying level with the ground, they fled with all the clergy that remained after so great a destruction to the coverts of the woods in Wales, and to Cornwall. [8] From this fact it is easily discernible how it came to pass that the Culdee or British Church has been associated to so great an extent with Wales and southern Scotland.

It has been said of the British Church that it made no effort to convert the Saxons to Christianity. In this connection several facts stand out very clearly; the Druidic religion had not yet died out in Britain and the Saxons found sufficient similarity between their own form of worship and that of ancient Britain to permit them to unite under the ministrations of a Druidic hierarchy, [9] deriving, it may be concluded, their religion from the same patriarchal source as the Druids.

The Druidic law of tithing was observed by the Anglo-Saxons, as by the Britons; the laws ascribed to Edward the Confessor speak of them as claimed by Augustine and conceded by the king, Ethelbert.

The Saxons looked with suspicion on efforts to

[7] "Annals of England," Vol. I, p. 164.

[8] Geoffrey of Monmouth, Bk. XI, ch. x.

[9] Palgrave, "Hist. of the Anglo-Saxons," p. 44.

convert them to Christianity by those whom they were endeavouring to subjugate, and were still non-Christian when in 597 the Augustinian mission, sent by Pope Gregory to introduce the Latin form of Christianity, reached these shores.

The civil power of Rome being dead, the ecclesiastical power began to rise on its ruins, and there may have been a connection between the two processes. The loss of one sphere of power may have helped to impel an ambitious people accustomed to universal dominion to seek after another sphere of power. The ambition of Pope Gregory became that also of the priest and delegate Augustine, to see the world brought under the sway of the fast developing kingdom of papal Rome, and when, in one day, Augustine baptised 10,000 Saxons the news of these "conversions" created great joy in Rome.

The immediate success achieved by Augustine in Kent so impressed Pope Gregory that he despatched more missionaries and with them church ornaments and vestments. Among these was the famous "pallium." This cloak, of ancient origin, the Roman emperors had been used to present to anyone whom they wished to mark with special honour. When the popes began to assume imperial authority, and to covet all the worldly splendour of the Caesars, they adopted the practice of bestowing the "pallium" on those whom they wished to elevate.

The arrival of the "pallium" in England for Augustine was a significant event. By favour of the Saxon king Ethelbert the Roman Church was set up at Canterbury; it became the chief seat of episcopal authority in England and was the origin of the Church known to-day as the Church of England. It will be observed that the origin of the British Church and that of the Church of England are quite distinct, with an interval of 560 years and the theory that Britain owes her Christianity to Augustine without foundation in fact.

The majority of the Saxons converted to Christianity in 597 soon gave evidence that their hearts were unchanged, they quickly fell away to their old religion. By 635 the Latin Church in Kent had become reduced to inactivity through continued hostilities between the Britons and Saxons, to be revived thirty years later when Roman practices and teaching were imposed on the British Church of Northumbria and to spread rapidly over the whole country.

There was already at Canterbury the British church built by St. Martin (traditionally the brother of St. Patrick's mother, Conessa), who founded also various churches in Scotland known as Kilmartin, and later that of Tours with which he has been historically associated. In passing, it should be noted that the British Church founded the churches of Gaul. The archbishops of Treves were, according to the Tungrensian Chronicles, always supplied from Britain. And coming nearer Rome itself, St. Cadval, a British missionary founded, A.D. 170, the church of Tarentum, after whom the cathedral at Tarento is still named.

The year 597, memorable alike for the death of Columba and the arrival of Augustine, has other worthy claims to notice. When Augustine came he found in the province of the Angles seven bishoprics and an archbishopric, all filled with most devout prelates, and a great number of abbeys.[10] The testimony of many writers, that the intrusion of an emissary of the Pope was resented and resisted by the British Church, is supported by facts of history.

At a Council held shortly after Augustine's arrival, he was told that "they knew no other Master than Christ," that "they liked not his new-fangled customs" and refused subjection.[11] Augustine angrily replied, "If we may not preach the way of life to you, you shall at the hands of your enemies (the Saxons) undergo their vengeance."[12]

The British Christians scorned the idea that identity in certain tenets and practices with papal Rome constituted the shadow of a title on the part of Rome to their allegiance. It is then no matter for surprise that on their first meeting with the delegate from Rome they should proclaim with one voice, "We have nothing to do with Rome: we know nothing of the Bishop of Rome in his new character of the Pope; we are the British Church, the Archbishop of which is accountable to God alone, having no superior on earth."

The Britons told Augustine they would not be subject to him, nor allow him to pervert the ancient laws of their Church. This was their resolution, and

---

[10] Geoffrey of Monmouth, Bk. XI, ch. xii.

[11] Brit. MSS. quoted in the second vol. of the Horæ Britannicæ, p. 267. Spelman's Concilia, p. 108.

[12] Bede, H. E., ch. ii, 2. Haddan & Stubbs, "Councils," iii, 38. Prof. J. E. Lloyd, "Hist. of Wales" (1911), p. 173.

they were as good as their word, for they maintained
the liberty of their Church five hundred years after
his time, and were the last of all the Churches of
Europe that gave up their power to Rome.[13] This
fact cannot be set aside as without significance in an
unprejudiced study of British Church history; Rome
found here a Church older than herself, ramifications
of which struck into the very heart of the continent
of Europe.   The further we go back into British
history, the clearer shines forth in all our laws the
entire independence of the British Crown, Church
and people, of all foreign authority.

All our great legal writers concur in this point.
"The ancient British Church," writes Sir William
Blackstone, "by whomsoever planted, was a stranger
to the Bishop of Rome, and all his pretended
authorities."[14]

The Christians of Britain could never understand
why, because the Church of Rome professed certain
truths, she should arrogate spiritual despotism over
all who held the same.   When Augustine demanded
of Dionoth, Abbot of Bangor Iscoed, or Bangor-on-
Dee, that he "acknowledge the authority of the
Bishop of Rome," the reply of the Briton is a
memorable one, "We desire to love all men, but he
whom you call 'pope' is not entitled to style himself
'the father of fathers' and the only submission we
can render him is that which we owe to every
Christian."[15]

[13] Bacon, "Government of England," p. 13.
[14] "Laws of England," Vol. IV, p. 105.
[15] Hengwrt MSS.   Geoffrey of Monmouth, Bk. XI, ch. xii.
Humphrey Llwyd, "Sebright MSS."

An ode, written in A.D. 540 by Ambrose Telesinas, a cleric of the British Church,[16] has these verses:

> "Woe to hym who doth nott keepe,
> From Romish woolves hys fflocks of sheepe
> And preach his charge amonge:
> Thatt will nott watch his fold alwai
> As toe his office doth belong.
> Woe to hym thatt doth nott keepe
> From Romish woolves his fflocke of Sheepe
> With staff and weapon strong."[17]

Cadvan, Prince of Wales, A.D. 610, expresses himself thus to the Abbot of Bangor: "All men may hold the same truths, yet no man hereby be drawn into slavery to another. If the Cymry believed all that Rome believed, that would be as strong reason for Rome obeying us, as for us to obey Rome. It suffices for us that we obey the Truth. If other men obey the Truth, are they therefore to become subject to us? Then were the Truth of Christ made slavery and not freedom."[18]

Wilfrid, a clever young priest, who had first been brought up in the school of Iona, but afterwards had travelled to Rome, and had become fascinated by her customs and grandeur, threatened in his long-drawn suit with the See of Canterbury to appeal to Rome in 670: the threat was received with laughter as a thing never before heard of in England.[19]

The British Church recognised the Apostolic

[16] "illustris presbyter Llandavaie." Geoffrey of Monmouth, ix, 15.
[17] Welsh Chronicles, p. 254.
[18] Caerwys MSS.
[19] Paton, "Brit. Hist. and Papal Claims," p. 4.

Scriptures alone for its rule of faith;[20] was subject to no other Church on earth, and firmly resisted the unwarranted intrusion of a pope. For almost two centuries Britain had been entirely free from the domination of Imperial Rome; this fact enabled the supporters of the British Church, at this time, to quote the second canon of the Council of Constantinople, held in A.D. 381, which ordained that "the Churches that are without the Roman empire should be governed by their ancient customs."[21] But this canon was not held sufficient by Augustine and his successors to justify the British Church in its contention.

Though the doctrinal controversies which divided the British and Roman Churches may seem unimportant to us, they plainly show our original ecclesiastical independence, and the stubborn resistance of our Church fathers to papal pretensions to supremacy.[22] Beyond all question to the national Church of Britain belongs that pre-eminence which the old British Triads claimed for it of being "primary in respect to Christianity."

The most famous of the English monasteries at the coming of Augustine was the monastery of Bangor-on-Dee, Wales.[23] Bishop Dionoth presided over a flourishing body of Christians (numbering some thousands) whose headquarters were at this

[20] Bede, "Eccles. Hist," Bk. III, ch. iv.

[21] Paper in the "Ecclesiastic" for April 1864 on Dr. Todd's "St. Patrick." "Concilio Constantiano" Theod. Martin (Lovar, 1517).

[22] M'Callum, "Hist. of the Culdees," pp. 60, 61.

[23] Ban-gor, "Magnus Circulus."

monastery of Bangor.[24] The youths there educated were trained in Christian doctrines, and sent forth as missionaries and teachers. Bangor, like Iona, was renowned for its zeal in propagating Christianity abroad. The refusal of its bishop, Dionoth, to acknowledge the authority of the Pope was the first of a long series of denials of the authority of Rome in Britain.[25]

At the Synod of Chester, held in 601, there were present, besides Augustine and some of his followers, seven British bishops and many men of great learning from the monastery of Bangor-on-Dee. Augustine at this Synod suffered a second defeat: the general assembly spoke out against the encroachments of Rome. "The Britons," they exclaimed, "cannot submit either to the haughtiness of the Romans, or the tyranny of the Saxons."[26]

Augustine did not live to take vengeance on these early protestors; it was left to his successor to lead the Saxons against them, and in the massacre of Bangor, A.D. 613, twelve hundred Christians perished.[27]

William of Malmesbury, A.D. 1143, describes the ruins of Bangor Abbey in his day as those of a city— the most extensive he had seen in the kingdom.[28] Two other foundations in England retained their superiority over all others of a later date, under

---

[24] MS. in the Mostyn Collection.

[25] MS. in the Mostyn Collection.

[26] "Annales Cambriae," CLVII.

[27] D'Aubigné, "Hist. Reform," Vol. V. Dean Milman, "Hist. of Latin Christianity," Vol. II, p. 234. "Annales Cambriae," CLXIX.

[28] Malmes "Hist. of the Kings," p. 308.

every change of rulers till the Reformation—
St. Alban and Glastonbury.

The next interference of papal Rome with British
customs took place in A.D. 664, the excuse for this
attempt being the correct date for the observance of
Easter.

King Oswy of Northumbria, with his brother
Oswald, were converted by missionaries from Iona,
while in exile for seventeen years in Scotland, during
the reign of the rival king, Edwin. Oswy adhered,
naturally, to the usages of the Culdee Church, having
been taught by the Scots. His queen, daughter of
Ethelbert, King of Kent, had been brought up to
observe the Latin way of reckoning, and each year
the strange anomaly occurred of the king and his
followers observing one day, and the queen observing
another day for the Easter festival.

The queen's chaplain, Romanus, and Wilfrid,
tutor to the princes, were priests of the Roman
Church, and urged the acknowledgment of the
Roman calculation for Easter as being correct. At
last the king resolved that the whole question should
be debated and settled once for all at a Synod of
Whitby. [29]

Bishop Colman (Culdee Church of Northumbria)
pleaded the British cause as having been derived from
his forefathers, and originated in the teaching of
St. John. Wilfrid, a cleverer man, was on the papal
side, and ridiculed British custom as compared with
that of the Apostle, "to whom Christ had given the
keys of Heaven." The king, eager to learn the truth,

[29] "Annales Cambriae," CCXXI. Bede, iii, 25.

enquired further into this statement; Colman, simple-minded and honest, admitted that these words applied to St. Peter. The king then asked Wilfrid whether Christ had really given the keys of authority to Peter. Wilfrid answered in the affirmative, whereupon the king decided in favour of the papal party. Colman resigned his bishopric, and with many of his clergy went back to Iona, from which monastery he had come to Northumbria, and where the ancient British Easter continued to be observed for many years.

From the day of the historic Synod of Whitby the province ruled by Oswy agreed to observe Easter the Latin way; and the British Church, though proved to be the oldest national Church in the world, as confirmed by the Councils of Arles, Basle, Pisa, Constance and Sena, was more and more coerced into conforming to papal customs and claims. For a time there were in Britain two Churches—the old British, the new Roman.

At the Council of Hertford, A.D. 673, but nine years after the Synod of Whitby, presided over by Archbishop Theodore, the British Church was condemned as non-Catholic.[30]

Wilfrid, at an assembly at Nesterfield, near Ripon, A.D. 703, declared: "Was not I the first after the death of those great men sent by St. Gregory, to root out the poisonous seeds sown by Scottish missionaries? Was it not I who converted and brought the whole nation of the Northumbrians to the true Easter and Roman tonsure?[31]

[30] Haddan & Stubbs, iii, pp. 258 ff.
[31] Montalembert, "Monks of the West," Vol. IV, p. 79.

In A.D. 705 Adelm wrote to the Britons as being
outside the "Catholic" Church; "the precepts of
your bishops," he says, "are not in accord with
Catholic faith[32] . . we adjure you not to persevere
in your arrogant contempt of the decrees of St. Peter,
and the traditions of the Roman Church, by a proud
and tyrannical attachment to the statutes of your
ancestors."[33]

The British Church, now openly declared heretical
by Rome, struggled on for a time as a separate
Church, and was known particularly from this time
by its original title, the "Culdee Church," as distinct
from the Roman, and its ecclesiastics were referred to
by the Latin intruders as the "British Clergy."

Adamnan, the first of the Ionian Culdees to
swerve from the faith, strained every nerve to reduce
the monks of Iona to Roman Catholic obedience.
Bede says that Adamnan, in A.D. 679, visited the
churches of Northumbria and Ireland and brought
almost all of them that were not under the dominion
of Hii (Iona) to the "Catholic" unity.

The resistance of the premier monastery (Iona),
the abbot of which was viewed as the Primate of all
the Hibernian bishops, prevailed for a time to retain
their liberties. By the eleventh century, however,
the Iona Church had become thoroughly Romanised
and had sunk into comparative unimportance.

Of Palladius, a Culdee of the fifth century, who
visited Rome and became a Romanising bishop,

---

[32] Adelmi opp., ed. Giles, pp. 24 ff. Monumenta Germ. Hist.
tom. iii, pp. 231 ff.

[33] "Monks of the West," Vol. IV, p. 233.

Fordun says: "Before whose coming the Scots had as teachers of the faith, and administrators of the sacraments, presbyters only and monks, following the order of the primitive Church."[34]

Kentigern (St. Mungo), A.D. 514, is numbered among those who adorned the name of Culdee; for many years he was the disciple of St. Servan at Culross, who taught and preached there as a Christian missionary, according to the system of the ancient British Church.

The Culdees or British clergy were, from Augustine's day, in constant collision with the Roman clergy; the Culdees seem to have been too much in love with simple Bible truth to find favour with those who aimed at wealth and power. Even the venerable Bede could not escape the prejudices of his "modern" times, saying: "The Culdees followed uncertain rules in the observation of the great festival (Easter), practising only such works of piety and chastity as they could learn from the prophetical, evangelical and apostolical writings."[35]

It is of consequence to note that in the early accounts which we have of the state of the Church, the final appeal in all doctrinal questions is to the Scriptures. It was remarked by Polydore Vergil that Gildas, in his long letter on the state of the Britons, quoted no book but the Bible;[36] and certainly his quotations from it show, on the part of the British historian, a very thorough acquaintance with the

[34] Scotichron., Lib. III, ch. viii.
[35] "Eccles. Hist.," III, ch. iv.
[36] "De Excid. Britt."

Word of God. At this period of the Church (fifth century) the Scriptures were very generally disseminated[37] and men used such translations of the sacred text as commended themselves to their own judgment. The withholding of the Bible from the people, and excluding every translation from use but the Latin translation, even among the ministers of the Church, belonged to the ecclesiastical legislation of a later and more corrupt age; an age when ecclesiastical power came to be based not on the intelligence, but on the ignorance, of the people.[38]

The Culdee or British Church had pervaded Britain with the knowledge of the Gospel, and for centuries after the domination of Rome the Culdees continued to hold services, frequently in the same church with Roman priests.

The catalogues of their books show beyond a doubt that the ancient British ecclesiastics were not destitute of literary culture.[39]

Corruption was powerfully retarded by the firmness of the hierarchy of the Culdees; they were looked up to as the depositaries of the original national faith, and were most highly respected for sanctity and learning. They acquired great missionary zeal, and great numbers of them went forth as missionaries and Christianised the whole of Europe from Iceland to the Danube;[40] this is a fact

[37] Williams, "Early Christianity in Britain," p. 447. Cephilos, Bishop of the Goths (A.D. 380), MS. in the Library of Upsal Naseau, viii, 40.

[38] *Vide* Ussher's "Historia Dogmatica."

[39] Keith Bish App., p. 5871. Regist. Priorat. St. Andree, p. xvii.

[40] Dasent, Introduction to "Burnt Njal," p. vii. "De Mensura Orbis," written by Dicuil, an Irish monk, in the year A.D. 825.

of history which has been diligently suppressed, but it is a fact which cannot be denied. It is remarkable that while the Church of Rome was sending her emissaries to "Christianise" the Saxons, the Celtic Church was sending her missionaries to convey the Gospel of Salvation to France.[41]

Dr. Wylie says: "It was the Culdee lamp that burned at Constance, at Basle, at Eprus, at Worms, and Mainz. Boniface, the emissary of Rome, came afterwards to put out these lights. The real apostle of the provinces was the Culdee Church."

A study of the history of the Culdees shows that wherever the influence of Rome prevailed they were removed; not, however, without resistance. But the struggle was a hopeless one. The Charter of David of Scotland (1084-1153), who was an adherent of the Latin Church, runs thus: "David rex Scotorum etc. Be it known, that we have granted to the Canons of St. Andrews the Island of Loch Leven, that they may establish there a Canonical Order; and if the Culdees who shall be found there, remain with them, living according to rule, they may continue to do so in peace; but if any one of them resist, we order hereby that he be ejected from the island."[42] In this high-handed manner was the property of the ancient Church transferred to the Roman hierarchy. Only a century before, Macbeth and his queen are recorded in the Register of this same Priory of

[41] D'Aubigné, "Hist. of the Reformation," Vol. IV. M'Lauchlan, "The Early Scottish Church," p. 216: "There was a Continental mission scheme in Scotland as early as 588."

[42] Registrum Prioratus St. Andree, p. 188. Keith Bish, p. 9.

St. Andrews as the liberal benefactors of the Culdee monastery at Loch Leven.

The property which the Culdees held in their own right was gradually confiscated by the Latin hierarchy, until the day came when they were dispossessed of everything, including their ancient privileges, and were absorbed into the Cathedral Chapters of the Roman Church. [43]

Ledwich, the Irish antiquarian, says: "The Culdees did not adopt the corruptions and superstitions which had contaminated Christianity for centuries. They preserved their countrymen from the baleful contagion, and at length fell a sacrifice in defence of the ancient faith. Superstition found in them her most determined foes. The Culdees continued until a new race of monks arose, as inferior to them in learning and piety, as they surpassed them in wealth and ceremonies, by which they captivated the eyes and infatuated the hearts of men. The conduct of the Romanisers towards the Culdees was uniformly persecuting; and by force, cunning and seduction of every kind, by degrees bereft them of their privileges and institutions." [44]

The monks of the papal Church were almost wholly employed in metaphysical or chronological disputes, legends, miracles and martyrologies—a sad contrast to the pure Scriptural teaching disseminated by the Culdees.

The history of the Culdee Church in Ireland was

[43] Alexander, "Ter-Centenary of the Scottish Reformation" (Edin., 1860), pp. 13, 17.
[44] Ledwich's "Antiquities."

largely the history of that Church in England,
Scotland and Wales, except that in the case of
Ireland she did not come, nationally, under the
domination of Rome until 1172, five centuries later
than in England. From this fact may be accounted
the theory held by many historians that the Culdee
and Irish Church were synonymous terms, and that
from it the Culdees spread to other parts of Britain, [45]
and further, it accounts for the strength of that
Church in Ireland centuries after its submission to
papal claims in England and elsewhere.

O'Driscoll, a noted Roman Catholic writer, states:
"The ancient order of the Culdees existed in Ireland
previous to Patrick; and all their institutions proved
that they were derived from a different origin from
that of Rome. This celebrated order gave many
eminent men to the Irish Church, and to Scotland
and other parts of the world, among whom Columb-
kill has still a name in Ireland as venerable and
revered as that of Patrick himself. The Church-
discipline of the Culdees seems to have afforded the
model for the modern Presbyterian establishment of
Scotland." [46]

The mission of Palladius, in A.D. 421, signally
failed. His effort to introduce papal Christianity in
Wicklow met with firm resistance and he shortly
afterwards left the country. [47]

The following year, St. Patrick, who belonged to
the Culdee Church, began his work as missionary

[45] *Vide* Reeve's "Culdees," p. 25.
[46] "Hist. of Ireland," pp. 26, 27.
[47] Bury, "Life of St. Patrick," pp. 54, 55.

revivalist. Christianity, according to Gildas, having been introduced to Ireland three and a half centuries earlier, and according to tradition, about the same date by Caradoc, the Silurian king, who, it is said, while a prisoner at Rome was converted to Christianity by St. Paul, and to whose children, Linus and Claudia, and his son-in-law, Pudens, St. Paul sends greetings in his second letter to Timothy.

From the days of St. Patrick to the reign of Henry II the Church in Ireland was renowned, not only for its learning and sanctity, but for its missionary zeal. Its evangelists spread the light of Truth where-ever they travelled in Britain, and to many places on the Continent, where the monasteries (afterwards Romanised) were set up on Culdee foundations, and to these many of the Culdee monks fled for refuge in the ninth and tenth centuries when Ireland was so sorely ravaged by the Danes. They took with them for safety many of their precious manuscripts, which may in a future day, should they be discovered, throw valuable light on the history of the early Christian Church in Britain.

O'Driscoll presents a true picture of the early Irish Church, when he says, "The Christian Church of that country as founded by St. Patrick existed for many centuries free and unshackled. For about seven hundred years this Church maintained its independence. It had no connection with England and differed on points of importance from Rome. The first work of Henry II was to reduce the Church of Ireland into obedience to the Roman Pontiff.

Accordingly he procured a Council of the Irish Clergy to be held at Cashel in 1172, and the combined influence and intrigues of Henry and the Pope prevailed. This Council put an end to the ancient Church of Ireland; she submitted to the yoke of Rome. This ominous apostasy has been followed by a series of calamities hardly to be equalled in the world. From the days of Patrick to the Council of Cashel was a bright and glorious career for Ireland. From the sitting of this Council to our own times the lot of Ireland has been unmixed evil and all her history a tale of woe." [48]

The following letter tells a curious story. It is from the Bishop of Mentz to Shane O'Neill, the Irish chief and rebel, dated from Rome, April 28th, 1528, in the name of the Pope and Cardinals: "My dear Son O'Neill,—Thou and thy fathers are all along faithful to the Mother Church of Rome. His Holiness Paul III, now Pope, and the Council of the Holy Fathers there, have lately found a prophecy of one St. Lazerianus, an Irish Bishop of Cashel, wherein he saith that the Mother Church of Rome falleth, when in Ireland the Catholic faith is overcome. Therefore, for the glory of the Mother Church, the honour of St. Peter, and your own secureness suppress heresy and his Holiness's enemies, for when the Roman faith there perisheth, the See of Rome falleth also. Therefore, the Council of Cardinals have thought fit to encourage your Country of Ireland, as a Sacred Island; being certified, whilst the Mother Church hath a son of

48 "Views of Ireland," Vol. II, p. 84.

worth as yourself, and those that shall succour you and join therein, that she will never fall, but have more or less hold in Britain, in spite of fate."[49] This letter was written in the reign of Henry VIII, at the time when the first indications were given to the Roman hierarchy of the mighty change about to take place in these realms.

[49] Mant's "Hist. of the Irish Church," p. 140.

CHAPTER XII

CULDEE INFLUENCE

It is on record that Culdees officiated in the Church of St. Peter, York, up to A.D. 936,[1] and according to Raine, the Canons of York were called Culdees as late as the reign of Henry II.

In the Cotton collection in the British Museum is preserved a Privilege which King Ethelred, A.D. 1016, is said to have granted to the Church of Canterbury, and Dr. Lingard, who first drew attention to the terms of the Privilege, observes that in the charters the prebendaries are termed "cultores clerici," which seems to indicate that the collegiate clergy were even then styled Culdees in the south as well as the north of England.[2]

In the tenth century, the Pictish king, Constantine II, according to the Register of St. Andrews, "having resigned the kingdom according to God's will he became Abbot of the Culdees at St. Andrews."[3]

The Culdees of St. Andrews continued long to form the chapter of the cathedral, and claimed the right of electing the bishop.[4]

From the same Register of St. Andrews we learn "The Culdees continued to perform divine worship

---

[1] Dugdale, "Monasticon Anglicanum," Vol. VI, Pt. ii, p. 607.
[2] "Hist. and Ant. of the Anglo-Saxon Church," ch. xiii (Vol. II, p. 294, ed. 1845).
[3] Innes, "Critical Essay," tom. II, p. 786.
[4] Regist. Priorat St. Andree, p. 49.

in a certain corner of the church after their own manner, nor could this evil be removed till the time of King Alexander in 1124, so that the Culdees and popish priests performed their services in the same church for nearly three hundred years."

Rev. C. G. Meissner says, "At the time of the Synod of Whitby the Christianity of Mercia was entirely Celtic in character; no Roman missionary had ever penetrated to the kingdom. . . . The Synod of Whitby left the position of the monastery of Lindisfarne absolutely unchanged, and not until 1138 did the last of those Celtic customs which had held their ground so tenaciously in the Church of Lindisfarne come to an end."[5] And Dr. W. Barry affirms, "Monks whose home was Iona or Lindisfarne helped to make England Christian from the Cheviots to the Thames. But Augustine, Paulinus and Wilfrid of York made it Roman in hierarchy, ritual and learning."[6]

The Culdees had in Abernethy a university and a collegiate church which is known to have subsisted toward the end of the thirteenth century,[7] and they were observed in Kyle and Cunningham until the followers of Wyckliff appeared, like the faint daybreak of the Reformation.

The following is an extract from a sermon of Bonars: "In some of the islands which we are apt to consider as the seat of ignorance and barbarism, lived a people remarkable for simplicity of manners,

---

[5] "Celtic Church," pp. 134, 158.
[6] "Papal Monarchy," p. 58.
[7]   Edin. Encyc., Vol. I.

purity of behaviour, and unaffected piety. Of their number were Columba and his brethren. Even in the tenth century when the darkness of corruption and error had grossly increased we are told there were some godly men in Scotland who taught the true doctrine of Christ's atonement and continued to receive their functions apart, without acknowledging the authority of those who assumed authority over God's inheritance."

Ledwich states that at Mondincha, in Tipperary, so late as 1185, a Culdean abbey and church still stood, "whose clergy had not conformed to the reigning superstition, but devoutly served God in this wild and dreary retreat, sacrificing all the flattering prospects of the world for their ancient doctrine and discipline. [8]"

Giraldus Cambrensis, who went to Ireland with King John, mentions the same abbey: "In North Munster is a lake containing two isles, in the lesser is a chapel where a few monks called Culdees devoutly serve God." [9]

Archbishop Ussher (1581-1656) says of these ecclesiastics of the ancient British Church: "In the greater Churches of Ulster, as at Cluanimnis (Clones) and Daminnis (Devenish) at Armagh, in our own memory, there were priests called Culdees who celebrated divine service in the Choir. Their president was styled Prior of the Culdees and acted as precentor." [10]

[8] "Irish Antiquities," pp. 102, 120.
[9] Topograph. Hibern. Dist. II, cap. iv (Camden's "Anglica," p. 716).
[10] "Britan. Eccles Antiq.," cap. xv (Works, Vol. VI, p. 174).

In Ireland the ancient title survived the Reformation and existed in the year 1628 when a deed was executed in which the lessor was "Edward Burton, prior of the Cathedral Church of Armagh, on behalf of the vicars choral and Culdees of the same."[11] Bishop Worth, in his rental of Killaloe drawn up in 1667, adds as a note on the thirty-three canons, "These in Ulster are called Culdees."[12]

It has been said that were we to search for that which most resembles the Culdee Church in modern times, we would find it in those great educational and mission establishments which the Scottish Churches have planted in India, where a body of earnest, enlightened men are engaged in teaching and preaching the Gospel, paying occasional visits to outlying towns and villages, and having occasional interviews with princes, for the purpose of communicating the knowledge of saving Truth.[13]

With all their imperfections, the Protestant Churches of Britain are the representatives of the original Christian or Culdee Church founded in these islands in apostolic times. Even in the "Dark Ages" Britain was never under the papacy to the extent that the Continental nations were.

If it were desired to strengthen from Roman Catholic documentary sources the Apostolical elements in the foundation of the British Church, or to insist that it can with equal justice, at least, with the Roman Church, claim St. Peter amongst its founders,

[11] Original in the Primate's Record Room, Armagh.
[12] Cotton's "Fasti Eccles. Hibern.," Vol. V, p. 66.
[13] McLauchlan, "The Early Scottish Church," p. 164.

it would not be difficult to adduce the affirmative evidence of Roman Catholic authorities upon the point. Cornelius à Lapide, in answering the question, "How came St. Paul not to salute St. Peter in his Epistle to the Romans?" states, "Peter, banished with the rest of the Jews from Rome, by the edict of Claudius, was absent in Britain";[14] and Eusebius Pamphilius, A.D. 306, quoted by Simeon Metaphrastes, states St. Peter to have been in Britain as well as in Rome.[16]

The discovery, at Whithorn, of the stone known as the "Peter Stone," seems to afford some support to the statements of these early writers. It is a rude pillar, four feet high and fifteen inches wide. An inscription in debased Roman capitals reads: "LOC(VS) S(ANC)TI PETRI APVSTOLI"—"The Place of St. Peter the Apostle." St. Peter would be, therefore, to the people of Britain, a Culdich or "refugee" from Rome in the reign of Claudius, A.D. 41-54, arriving in Britain a few years after the arrival of the "Judean refugees" or Culdich (certain strangers) from Palestine in the last year of Tiberius, A.D. 37.

The vision to which St. Peter refers (2 Peter i, 14), "Knowing that shortly I must put off this my tabernacle, even as our Lord Jesus Christ hath shewed me," is said to have appeared to him in Britain on the spot where once stood the British Church of Lambedr (St. Peter) and now stands the Abbey of St. Peter's, Westminster.[16]

[14] Cornelius à Lapide, in "Argum Epist St. Pauli ad Romanos," ch. xvi.
[16] Metaphrastes ad 29 Junii. Menologii Graecorum.
[14] Dean Stanley, "Mem. of Westminster Abbey," ch. i, p. 18.

In considering evidence in support of the belief that St. Paul visited Britain, it is of consequence to note that the tradition that he did so has been accepted by numerous writers, including Ussher and Stillingfleet.[17]

In the fourth century Theodoret wrote, "St. Paul brought salvation to the isles in the ocean,"[18] and also mentions the Britons among the converts of the apostles. And in the same century Jerome states that St. Paul's evangelical labours extended to the western parts.

In the sixth century Venantius, and in the seventh the Patriarch of Jerusalem, speak expressly of St. Paul's mission to Britain.[19]

After the Synod of Whitby, the whole organisation of the British Church was gradually remodelled, so that it would be exceedingly difficult to recognise the old Church of the first five centuries in the great hierarchial establishments of the Church of Rome. In the course of time, instead of the unpretentious Culdee establishment, arose a powerful hierarchy, the members of which came to hold the highest offices in Church and State. This change in the Church, accompanied with the accumulation of wealth by rich endowments, and the high offices often being filled by foreigners, was repugnant to the native population, who had long bravely defended their country, and filled the offices in Church and State well, and who were now put aside, their liberties withheld and their property confiscated.

[17] *See* Rev. W. Hughes, "Church of the Cymry," p. 13.
[18] "Intepr. in Psalm 116," opp Lut. Par. 1642.
[19] Ussher, "Brit. Eccl. Antiq.," p. 4.

Conquerors are not usually disposed to speak with much kindness or respect of those whom they have overcome or dispossessed. It was so between the successful priests of the Roman hierarchy and the ecclesiastics of the ancient Church of the Culdees, whom they had succeeded in supplanting. But it is significant that the British continued in after times to cherish the highest esteem for the memory of these men of piety and power who had distinguished their ancient national church. Rome might have supplanted the Culdee Church; she could not eradicate from the minds of the people the principles it had imparted.

It requires but little acquaintance with British history to observe that these principles never were eradicated, that during the reign of the Roman Church in these islands they continued to exist. Men like Alcuin in his Caroline books, John Scotus, the protége of King Alfred, and Archbishop Elfric with his "Saxon Homily," endeavoured to stem the incoming tide of doctrinal error

King Alfred, a great patron of literature, gave to his people, in the ninth century, the Gospels in the Saxon tongue—a life work worthy of record. We find from a letter of King Alfred that he wrote: "I wish you to know that it often occurs to my mind to consider what manner of wise men there were formerly in the British nation, both spiritual and temporal. I considered how earnest God's ministers then were, as well about preaching as about learning in this land." [20]

[20] Aelfred praef. ad Past., 85. Nicephorus, ii, 40.

Continual friction and frequent outbursts of resistance to Roman encroachments marked the whole period of Rome's attempted domination in Britain, and are exhibited in such outbreaks as the letter of King Robert Bruce and his nobles to Pope John, the uprising of the Lollards, and finally the events of the Reformation. British independence, civil and ecclesiastical, is well expressed in the words of Robert Bruce: "It is not Glory: it is not Riches: neither is it Honour; but it is Liberty alone that we fight and contend for, which no honest man will lose but with his life." [21]

Edgar the Pacific, A.D. 959 to 975, fearlessly proclaimed in the presence of Dunstan (first of the great ecclesiastical statesmen of whom Wolsey was the last), and with the enthusiastic approval of his nobles and the nation, as claiming no novelty, but their immemorial right and liberty, "That the King of England held the Sword of Constantine, that he was in his own dominions the Lord's Husbandman, the Pastor of pastors, and the representative of Christ on Earth." [22]

The Roman hierarchy, it is now evident, actuated by such zeal against the Culdees, has not allowed them common historical justice. Their influence, however, remained and these early protesters against a Romanised Church in these islands, lived and worked through evil report and good report, until the time in which the followers of Wyckliff appeared.

The love of the Scriptures, to which the Culdees

[21] T. Wright, "Hist. of Scot.," Vol. I, p. 111.
[22] Twysden, "Scriptores," x, p. 360.

had trained the people, never entirely died out. To the early British or Culdee Church our country owes its Protestantism: its determination to exercise individual freedom in religion: its love of the Scriptures and its missionary zeal.

> "The pure Culdees
> Were Albyn's earliest priests of God,
> Ere yet an island of her seas
> By foot of Saxon monk was trod."
>
> *Campbell*, "Reullura."

CHAPTER XIII

THE REFORMATION

A VERY common knowledge of history, a very little research would suffice to prove that the work of the Culdees, who became, from the first encroachment of Rome, the British protesters, never quite died out, and that the Reformation in these islands began long anterior to the date usually assigned to it. It was the struggle for religious rights which opened men's eyes to all their rights. It was resistance to religious usurpation which led men to withstand political oppression.

The first notable resistance to the papacy as a step towards the Reformation was made by William the Conqueror. When Pope Gregory VII demanded homage of the king for his realm of England, William replied: "Fealty I have never willed to do, nor will I do it now. I have never promised it, nor do I find that my predecessors did it to yours."[1]

William never permitted his clergy to be governed by the will of the Pope, and when Lanfranc, Archbishop of Canterbury, was summoned by that dignitary to appear before him at Rome to answer for the rebellious conduct of the English king, William refused to let him proceed.[2]

---

[1] Green, "Short Hist. of the Eng. People," ch. ii, p. 83.
[2] Freeman, "Nor. Conq.," Vol. IV, pp. 434, 435. Hume, "Hist. of England," Vol. I, p. 361.

William never bowed before the papacy, yet we must not make the mistake of thinking him a Protestant as we now understand the term. While he overcame all papal attempts to gain political ascendancy in England, the spiritual power of the Latin Church remained for centuries the dominant, though waning, power in this country.

Along with the fact that the Culdees existed down to the days of Wyckliff should be placed the statement that it was said in his day, "You could not meet two men on the road but one was a Wyckliffite." The Reformation commenced in England, Wyckliff being 136 years earlier than Luther, and probably half the nation went with him.

While Wyckliff was translating the Scriptures, and preparing the way for Reformation principles, another reformer in the person of Edward III was taking the first steps towards the sweeping away of papal jurisdiction from the national Church.

Edward III, following in the footsteps of the British king, Arthur, the founder of the "Round Table," whom he appears to have made his ideal, identified himself all through his reign with the interests of the national Church against the encroaching claims of the Roman See.[3] The threat of the Pope to cite him to appear at his Court of Avignon to answer for his defaults in not performing the homage, nor paying the tribute to the See of Rome, undertaken and guaranteed by John, King of England, for himself and his heirs, was submitted by Edward to Parliament for their advice: it was given by the

---

[3] Moberley, "Life of Wm. Wykeham," p. 175.

Bishops, Lords and Commons, after full deliberation, in the following memorable words: "That neither King John nor any other king could bring himself, his realm and people under such subjection without their assent . . . that if done, it was without the consent of Parliament and contrary to his coronation oath, and that in case the Pope should attempt to constrain the King and his Subjects to perform what he lays claim to, they would resist and withstand him to the uttermost of their power." [4]

Instructing his chaplain, William of Wykeham, who was also his surveyor and secretary, to make enquiries into the tradition of the Order of St. George and the Garter, it was revealed that the British Church of the first five centuries had been entirely free from papal control, and that one of the first acts of Arthur's reign had been to refuse the tribute demanded by special emissaries sent from Rome. It may have been this precedent set by his predecessor that determined King Edward to obtain a Bull from Pope Clement VI (1348) declaring the Chapel of St. George a free chapel, that is, free, as had been the early British Church, from papal jurisdiction.

The Sovereign—the head of the Order—and the Bishop of Winchester, the Prelate, nominated the deans and canons, with appeal to the visitor, the Lord Chancellor.

The Royal Chapel of St. George, Windsor, may, therefore, claim to be the foundation stone of the Reformation, and as a religious foundation thoroughly organised in every detail of its constitution by fifty-

[4] Hansard, "Parl. Records," Vol. I, p. 129.

four original statutes. St. George's College is the first in England founded "free" of the control of abbot or prior, and its statutes have been the model upon which all post-Reformation and collegiate staffs have been moulded.

The Marquis of Lorne, Constable of Windsor Castle, reminds us that Windsor takes precedence of Westminster Abbey, and that the succession of deans and canons of Windsor has not been interrupted for five and a half centuries.[5]

Edward III may be said to have begun the resistance to the Roman claims to supremacy, which culminated in the final secession under Henry VIII two hundred years later.

The Duke of Lancaster, known to history as "John of Gaunt," son of Edward III, feudal to the core, resented the official arrogance of the prelates and the large share which they drew to themselves of the temporal power, and made alliance with Wyckliff, who dreamed of restoring by apostolic poverty its long-lost apostolic purity to the clergy. From points so opposite and with aims so contradictory were they united to reduce the wealth and humble the pride of the Roman hierarchy.

Another factor which gave a tremendous impetus to the work of purification from the errors of Rome was the economic difficulties in the days of Wyckliff, caused by the "Black Death" which prepared the hearts of the people to receive a reformed Christian religion.

Dean Milman, a nineteenth century scholar, says

[5] "Governor's Guide," 8vo., London, 1897.

K—c

(with regard to "Piers the Ploughman," written about this time, A.D. 1362, by William Langlande), "The people who could listen with delight to such strains were far advanced towards a revolt from Latin Christianity. Truth, true religion was not to be found with, it was not known by Pope, Cardinals Bishops, Clergy, Monks or Friars. It was to be sought by man himself, by the individual man, by the poorest man, under the sole guidance of Reason, Conscience, and the Grace of God, vouchsafed directly, not through any intermediate human being or even sacrament, to the self-directing soul. There is a manifest appeal throughout, an unconscious installation of Scripture alone, as the final judge."[6]

The petty revenge of Rome in taking up the remains of Wyckliff in 1428, forty-four years after his death, and casting them into the waters of the Swift, served only to add a new lustre to the fame of the reformer. As the historian, Thomas Fuller, says: "The little river conveyed Wyckliff's remains into the Avon, the Avon into the Severn, the Severn into the narrow seas, and they into the main ocean. And thus the ashes of Wyckliff are the emblem of his doctrine which now is dispersed all over the world."[7]

Huss had received the light from Wyckliff, and he with his co-workers, Jerome, Latimer and Ridley, and Wyckliff's followers, the Lollards, were links in the chain between Wyckliff and the Reformation.

The protest against the supremacy of the Pope in this land, based on the laws of the kingdom, was

[6] "Hist. of Latin Christianity," Vol. II, p. 234.
[7] "Church Hist. of Britain," Vol. II, p. 424.

another cause which impelled Britain towards the day of Reformation. The glorious day of fuller light and liberty was, however, far off. Ignorance was widespread, and its saddest phase was the decay of knowledge of the Word of God. The Bible was locked up from the people because it was written in Hebrew, Greek or the Latin into which Jerome had translated the Scriptures. The unlearned people had no power whereby to open the divine treasure-house until they were given the Bible in the English language.

The clergy also, with the laity, appear to have been in great ignorance concerning the Scriptures. Rome well knew that reading the Bible intelligently stimulates enquiry, extends the realm of thought and emancipates the mind from slavery to mere human authority.

In the time of Pope Alexander VI (1492) so ignorant were some of the clergy that a French monk said: "They have now found out a new language called Greek; we must carefully guard ourselves against it. That language will be the mother of all sorts of heresies. I see in the hands of a great number of persons a book written in this language, called 'The New Testament'; it is a book full of brambles, with vipers in them. As to the Hebrew, whoever learns that becomes a Jew at once." [8]

We read in Luther's "Table Talk" of an Archbishop of Mainz coming across a copy of the Bible, and on examining it was quite puzzled as to what it could be. When he began to read it he was so taken

[8] Sismondis, "Hist. des Francais," xvi, 364.

aback that he exclaimed: "Of a truth, I do not know what book this is, but I perceive everything in it is against us."

With the invention of printing in the late fifteenth century, the preaching and writings of the Reformers were gradually spread among the people, not, however, without raising the opposition of the Roman hierarchy.

The Vicar of Croydon, preaching at St. Paul's Cross in the days of Henry VIII, declared that either the Roman Church must abolish printing or printing would abolish her!

Caxton's press was established in the almonry at Westminster, a little enclosure containing a chapel and alms-houses. A red pole showed the seeker where the printed books could be bought "good chepe." Not the people only, but kings favoured the wonderful new process. Rome alone discouraged it. At her General Council in 1514 she forbade the printing of any books, except with her permission.

About this time several translations of the Scriptures were printed and circulated. Miles Coverdale assisted Tyndale in re-translating the Pentateuch about 1530, and shortly afterwards, in 1535, appeared his own translation of the Bible. Two years later, 1537, another translation appeared —that of John Rogers, the Martyr, and in 1539, the translation of Taverner, another Cambridge man. Rogers was the first to be brought to the stake in the five dark years of Mary's reign.

One of the most interesting events of Edward VI's short reign was the publication of the second prayer book. Many of the imperfections of the first prayer book were removed, its dross more thoroughly purged away, and the result—with some further revision in Elizabeth's reign—is the "Book of Common Prayer" used to-day in the English Church Services.

With the passing of Mary of England, and the accession of Queen Elizabeth, came the feeling throughout the land that brighter days had dawned; imprisoned witnesses for the Faith were freed with the joyful assurance that the reign of the stake was over.

The long reign of Queen Elizabeth was noted for the overthrow of every concession to the papacy. She sincerely resolved to restore Protestantism (the Reformation having been definitely begun by Edward VI and interrupted during Mary's reign), but the work was attended with serious dangers. Most of the clergy were papists, for the notable and learned divines and Gospel preachers had passed away in fiery martyrdom.

Yet in spite of all difficulties, Elizabeth kept on her course without flinching. One of her first acts was to forbid the elevation of the Host at the Mass, to enjoin that the Litany, Epistle and the Gospel be read in English, and that all preaching be forbidden except by those who had obtained special licence. The necessity for this step was that as the majority of the clergy were papists, sermons against the reformed doctrines would have been preached had they been permitted.

When the Archbishop of York, Nicholas Heath,

who refused to take the oath of supremacy, exhorted Elizabeth to follow the Pope, she gave him a memorable reply: "I will answer you in the words of Joshua. As Joshua said of himself and his: 'I and my realm will serve the Lord.' My sister (Mary) could not bind the realm, nor bind those who should come after her, to submit to a usurped authority. I take those who maintain here the Bishop of Rome, and his ambitious pretensions, to be enemies to God and to me." [9]

The Elizabethan "Act of Uniformity" enjoined all ministers "to say, and use, the Matins, Evensong, Celebrations of the Lord's Supper, etc., as authorised by Parliament in the fifth and sixth year of Edward VI." This Act, aimed only against papists, became afterwards a bitter yoke to many Protestants.

A large Bible, a Book of Homilies, and Erasmus's "Paraphrase of the New Testament" were ordered to be placed in every church at the expense of the parish; while Sunday after Sunday the reading of the Scriptures in English and of the Homilies was gradually enlightening those who sat in darkness.

The progress of the Reformation received every encouragement from those exiles who had taken refuge in Zurich, Geneva and Strasbourg, but now returned to England when they heard that the black night had passed away. Among them must be mentioned Bishop Jewel, the author of the famous work entitled "The Apology of the Church of England." It was written in Latin because it was addressed to all Europe, and as the answer of the

' Strype, "Annals," Vol. I, pp. 207, 208.

Reformed National Church of England to those
Roman Catholics who said that the Reformation had
set up a new Church. Jewel rightly contended that
the Reformers were returning to the primitive Church
of the first century, as founded by the Apostles, and
was not in any way a "novel" Church.[10]

As in England, so in Ireland, the yoke of Rome was
cast aside by the National Church at the Reformation. The Very Rev. R. G. S. King, M.A., Dean of
Derry, in his brochure on St. Patrick, states: "When
Elizabeth was carrying out the Reformation, ten of
the Irish bishops had been bishops under Henry VIII.
If you had told them they belonged to a new Church
they simply would not have understood you.
Removal of abuses nor changes in a Prayer Book do
not make a new Church. . . . The simple historical
truth is there was no break in the continuity of the
Church of Ireland at the Reformation, and every
attempt to prove the contrary has only resulted in
confirmation of its unbroken descent from the
ancient Church of our native land."

Thus the Reformation was established, though
not perfected, in the days of Elizabeth, and the yoke
of Rome imposed unwittingly by King Oswy in
A.D. 664 was thrown aside nine centuries later by
Queen Elizabeth, and the cleansing of the sanctuary
begun.

On one occasion, in a speech before Parliament,
Queen Elizabeth said: "Thus much I must say, that
some faults and negligences may grow and be in the
Church, whose over-ruler God hath made me. . . .

[10] "Ap. Ch. of England," pp. 13, 14.

All which, if you, my lords of the clergy, do not amend, I mean to depose you. Look you, therefore, well to your charges."[11]

It was a determined policy of Queen Elizabeth to put a period to papal intrusion upon her authority in her realm, and in the pursuit of this policy many papists suffered death for political offences. Religious persecution, however, occupied no place in Elizabeth's policy, and it was her joyful boast that no Romanist had been put to death during her reign on account of his religion. Whatever may be said to lessen in this respect the contrast favourable to this reign in comparison with the previous reign, it is sufficiently marked to be thoroughly appreciated by all but the prejudiced.

The character of the early British Church was now in a great measure restored. It must not be forgotten, however, that the Church at no time was without its protesters, the Culdees, worshipping God according to the practices of the primitive Church in these islands, and frequently in the same Church with Latin priests. As related in the previous chapter, they were known to have existed down to the seventeenth century.

From the Reformation onwards the Protestant Church did not maintain that intense zeal which her earlier supporters displayed; apathy crept in, divisions and sub-divisions occurred, weakening her cause throughout the land.

As early as 1689, a desire for unity in Protestantism was expressed by Archbishop Sancroft, in an

[11] Hansard, "Parl. Records," Vol. I, p. 833.

admonition to his clergy, and in his own "very tender regard to our brethren the Protestant Dissenters." He exhorts his clergy to "take all opportunities of assuring these non-conforming brethren that the Bishops of this Church are really and sincerely irreconciliable enemies to the errors of the Church of Rome, and that the very unkind jealousies which some have had of us to the contrary were altogether groundless. And, in the last place, that they warmly and most affectionately exhort them to join with us in daily fervent prayer to the God of peace, for the universal blessed union of all Reformed Churches, both at home and abroad against our common enemies, that all they who do confess the holy name of our dear Lord, and do agree in the truth of His Holy Word, may also meet in one holy communion, and live in perfect unity and godly love."[12]

It has been said that the Episcopalian, the Presbyterian and the Independent can each discover in the early British Church the prototype of the system to which he adheres. Paton supports this view when he says: "If the question be asked was the organisation of the Celtic Church in Scotland Presbyterian or Episcopalian, the answer of an impartial judge must be that it was neither the one nor the other, but an order, *sui generis*—a system of Church polity which might develop into either, or even into something different from both." It has also been said that the Elizabethan Church might, in the seventeenth century, have retained the Puritans if

[12] Life, p, 196.

it had been wisely led. The saintship of the laity is the secret of the Puritan faith, and it is something that is vital to British Christianity.

Each denomination of Protestantism has behind it, at least, this common principle, the intention to be true to the purpose of Our Lord as it was unfolded in the Apostolic writings.

There is much in the past history of the British nation for the thoughtful Protestant to study. The truth, however, does not lie on the surface. On the confession of Roman Catholic historians themselves our histories, both civil and ecclesiastical, have been written with an astonishing indifference to truth.

Dr. Barry, a historian of the Latin Church, says: "To manipulate ancient writings, to edit history in one's own favour, did not appear criminal—in the ages of faith—if the end in view were otherwise just and good";[13] and Cardinal Newman, to whom a proposal had been made to found a Roman Catholic Historical Review, replied: "Who could bear it, unless one doctored all one's facts one would be thought a bad Catholic."[14]

The undisputed writings of the early Christians begin about seventy years after the time of the Apostles. At that period there probably remained none of the first converts or contemporaries of the Apostles. But there were living not a few who had been acquainted with the last survivors of that generation. When the Apostles died they must have left behind them a multitude who had known them.

[13] "Papal Monarchy," p. 133.
[14] "The Month," Jan. 1903, p. 3.

And of these not a few must have continued many years, and must have had intercourse with the new generation which sprang up after the Apostolic age. In the time of this generation the series of Christian authors begins, and they testify to the establishment of a Christian Church in Britain. The story of this British Church is the story of the Light that never went out.

Montalembert's appreciation of the British nation and her religion is summed up in the following words: "After enduring as much and more than any European nation the horrors of religious and political despotism in the sixteenth and seventeenth centuries, she has been the first and the only one among them to free herself from oppression forever. Re-established in her ancient rights, her proud and steadfast nature has forbidden her since then to give up into any hands whatsoever her rights and destinies, her interests and her free will. In spite of a thousand false conclusions, a thousand excesses, a thousand stains, she is of all modern races and of all Christian nations the one which has best preserved the three fundamental bases of every society which is worthy of man—the spirit of freedom, the domestic character and the religious mind. The Christianity of nearly half the world flows, or will flow, from the fountain which first burst forth upon British soil."[16]

The Gospel sown by the first Culdees in the soil prepared for its reception by the labours, for centuries, of Druidism now yields a mighty harvest throughout the English-speaking world.

[16] "Monks of the West," Vol. II, p. 367.

Travelling swiftly through uncharted periods of Britain's religious history, and up to the Reformation, a mere glance is all that has been possible in this small volume, at some of the outstanding events which have left so indelible a mark upon British character; approach by various avenues has been suggested, any or all of which would lead to illuminating facts in support of lesser-known truths of our history, and to a possible awakening to the responsibilities of a great and ancient heritage.

BIBLIOGRAPHY

Adonellus (Manus 'O'Donnell) Vita Columbae, 109
Ailred Vita Niniani, 107
Alexander, William Lindsay Tercentenary of the Scottish Reformation, 128
Alfred, King Praef. ad Pastoral, 139
Allard, Paul La Persecution de Diocletian, 104
Allen, Romilly Celtic Art, 28
Ammianus Marcellus Historia, 26, 51
Ancient Laws of Cambria (Brit. Mus.) 20, 21, 24, 61
Annals of England (1855-57) 114
Armagh, Book of 67
Arnobius Commentary on the Psalms, 91
Arnold, Matthew Celtic Literature, 48, 72, 81
Athenagoras An Embassy, 75
Avienus, Festus Orc Maritama, 27

Bacon, Nathaniel Laws and Government of England, 93, 118
Baker MSS., Cambridge 23
Barry, Dr. W. Papal Monarchy, 134, 154
Bede Ecclesiastical History, 107, 117, 120, 122, 125
Blackstone, Sir William Commentaries on the Laws of England, 118
Boece, Hector Scotorium Historiae (ed. J. Bellenden), 110
Bouche Defense de la Foi de Provence pour ses Saints, 88
Bower, Walter Scotichronicon, 125
Bracton, Henry de Legibus et Consuet, 22

Note.—There are English translations of the Life of Agricola by Tacitus (his son-in-law), Life of St. Columba (Adamnan), Diodorus Siculus and some other works quoted herein. Librarians and Educational Booksellers will give details.

Browne, C. F., D.D. — The Christian Church before the Coming of Augustine, 75

Bury, John Bagnall, D.D. — St. Patrick, 129

Caesar — Commentarii De Bello Gallico, 50, 51, 54, 64

Caerwys, MSS. — 119
Camden, William — Anglica Hibernica, 39
Campion, Edmund — An Account of Ireland, 50
Carte, Thomas — History of England, 55
Cave, William — Historia Literaria, 17
Chadwick, H. Monro — Origin of the English, 113
Chronicum Regum Pictorum — 16
Chrysostomi — Orat a Theo Xristus, 91
Cirencester, Richard of — Ancient State of Britain, 40
Cleland, John — Ancient Celtica, 74
Coke, Sir Edward — Pleadings, 20
Colgan, John — Trias Thaumaturga, 87
Collier, Jeremy — Ecclesiastical History, 40
Collingwood, R. C. — Archaeology of Roman Britain, 28

Cormac, Archbishop — Irish Lexicon, 67
Cotton, Henry — Fasti Ecclesiae Hibernicae, 136

Cottonian, MSS. — 106
Cunnington, R. H. — Stonehenge and its Date, 80
Cusack, M. F. — History of the Irish Nation, 60, 71, 73

Cyprian — Epistles, 100

Dalrymple, Sir James — Historic Collections, 103
Dasent, Sir George — Burnt Njal, 126
D'Aubigné, J. H. M. — History of the Reformation, 121, 127

Davies, Rev. Edward — Celtic Researches, 46
    „   „   „ — Mythology and Rites of the British Druids, 64
Davies, J. B. — Crania Britannicae, 62
Discuil — Liber de Mensura Orbis Terrae, 126

Diodorus Siculus — Bibliotheca Historica, 25, 29, 55, 61

Dion Cassius (Xiphilinus Excerpta) — Monumenta Britannica, 31, 36, 37

Domesday Survey — 88

Donnelly, Ignatius — Atlantis, 54

D'Oyly, George, D.D. — Life of Archbishop Sancroft, 153

Dugdale, Sir William — Monasticon Anglicanum, 100, 133

Encyclopaedia Britannica, 11th edition — 108

Edinburgh Encyclopaedia — 134

Eumenius — Panegyric on Constantius, 29

Eusebius of Caesarea — Demonstratione Evangelii, 90

„ „ „ — On Socrates, 105

Evans, Sir John — Coins of the Ancient Britons, 29

Fergusson, James — History of Architecture, 56

Fergusson, Lady — The Irish before the Conquest, 71

Fontenu, Abbé de — Mem. de Litterature, 26

Fordun, John — Scotichronicon, 125

Fortescue, Sir John — De Laudibus Legum Angliae, 20

Freculphus, Bishop — Chronicon, apud Godwin de Presulibus, 87

Freeman, E. A. — Norman Conquest, 15, 142

Fryer, A. C. — Llantwit Major, 106

Fuller, Thomas — Church History of Britain, 103, 104, 146

Gibbon, Edward — Decline and Fall of the Roman Empire, 84

Gibson, Dr. Edmund — Camden, 32

Gildas — De Excidio Britanniae, 90, 101, 104, 125

„ — M.S. Cottonian Library, 49

Giles, J. A. — Adelmi, 124

Giraldus Cambrensis — Cambriae Descript, 18

„ „ — Topograph. Hibern. Distinct. 95, 100, 135

Godwin, Francis	De Presulibus, 65, 87
Gordon, E. O.	Prehistoric London, 23
Green, J. R.	Short History of the English People, 142
Grimm, Jac.	Deutsche Sagen, 112
Haddan and Stubbs	Councils and Ecclesiastical Documents, 104, 107, 117, 123
Hannay, H. Bruce	European and other Race Origins, 16, 113
Hansard, Luke	Parliamentary Records, 144, 152
Hengwrt, M. S. S.	118
Henry, Robert D. D.	History of Great Britain, 51, 65
Herodotus	Thalia, 29
Hilary of Poictiers	De Synodis, 106
Hoare, Sir R. Colt	Ancient Wilts, 32
Holinshed, Richard	Chronicles of England, Scotland and Ireland, 22, 67, 92
Holmes, T. Rice	Ancient Britain, 27
Home, Gordon	Roman York, 29
Hughes, J.	Horae Britannica, 117
Hughes, Rev. W.	Church of the Cymry, 67, 138
Hulbert, Charles	Religions of Britain, 62
Hume, David	History of England, 57, 142
Huntingdon, Henry of	Historia Anglorum, 62
Huxley, Thomas	Forefathers and Forerunners of the British People. Anthrop. Rev. (1870), 15
Hyppolytus	Philisophumena, 51
Innes, Thomas	Critical Essay on the Ancient Inhabitants of Scotland, 133
James, Rev. D.	Patriarchal Religion, 67
Jamieson, John D.D.	History of the Culdees, 101, 102
Jewel, Bishop	Apology of the Church of England, 151

Jerome	Comment on Isaiah, 91
Josephus	Antiquities, 61
,,	Jewish Wars, 59
Juvenal	Satires, 25
Keith, R.	Catalogue of the Scottish Bishops, 126, 127
King, Daniel (W. Webb)	Vale Royal, 60, 94
King, The Very Rev. R. G. S.	
King, M.A.	151
Laertius. Diogenes (F. Nietzche)	Proemium, 46, 47
Laing, Samuel	Heimskringla, 113
Lapide, Cornelius à	Epist. St. Pauli ad Romanos, 137
Latham, Dr. R. G.	Ethnology of the British Islands, 15
Lecain, Book of	53
Ledwich, Rev. Edward	Irish Antiquities, 128, 135
Lewis, Sir G. C.	Astronomy of the Ancients, 55
Lewis, Samuel	History of Britain, 23, 62
Lingard, John	History of the Anglo-Saxon Church, 133
Llandâv, Book of	93, 100
Lloyd, Prof. J. E.	History of Wales, 48, 117
Llwyd, A.	Island of Mona, 59, 108
Llwyd, Humphrey	History of Cambria, 118
Lockyer, Sir Norman	Stonehenge, 54, 58, 64
Lorne, Marquis of (Duke of Argyll)	Governors Guide to Windsor Castle, 145
Lucanus	Pharsalia, 57, 64
Lumisden, Andrew	Antiquities of Rome, 19
Lysons, Samuel	Our British Ancestors, 30, 53, 59
Lytton, Lord	King Arthur, 82
Maclear, Rev. G. F., D.D.	Conversion of the West. The Celts, 67
McCallum, D.	History of the Culdees, 88, 100, 101, 120
MacCuillinan, Cormac	Psalter of Cashel, 16

McLauchlan, Rev. T., M.A.	The Early Scottish Church, 87, 127, 136
Macpherson, J.	Dissertations (Fingal), 47, 101
Maine, Sir Henry	Early Irish Institutions, 73
Malmesbury, William of	History of the Kings, 90, 121
Mansi, G. D.	Councils, 105
Mant, Richard	History of the Irish Church, 132
Margoliouth, Moses	Jews in Britain, 65
Martial	Epigrams, 32, 40
Massey, Gerald	The Book of Beginnings, 84
Maurice, Thomas	Indian Antiquities, 63
Meissner, Rev. R. G., M.A.	The Celtic Church in England after the Synod of Whitby, 134
Mela Pomponius	De Situ Orbis, 19, 51, 54, 64
Menologii Graecorum	137
Metaphrastes, Simeon	Junii, 137
Milman, Henry Hart, D.D.	History of Latin Christianity, 121; 146
Milton, John	History of England, 18
Moberley, G. H.	William of Wykeham, 143
Mommsen	Monumenta Germaniae Historica, 124
Monceaus, Abbat of Atrebas	Syntagma Theologiae, 93
Monmouth, Geoffrey of	History of Britain, 17, 22, 114, 117, 118, 119
Monro, Donald	Miscell. Scotica, 102
Montalembert, C. F. R.	Monks of the West, 45, 69, 109, 123, 124, 155
Moore, Thomas	History of Ireland, 72
Morgan, Rev. M. W.	British Cymry, 49, 93
Morgan, Rev. R. W.	St. Paul in Britain, 35, 40, 95, 105
Mostyn, M.S.S.	121
Muller, Prof. Max.	Selected Essays, 82
Mylne, Alexander	History of the Bishops of Dunkeld, 88
Nash, D. W.	Taliesen, Bards and Druids of Britain, 61
Nennius	Historia Britannicae, 17, 18, 93

Newman, Cardinal — The Month, 154

Nicholas, Thomas, M.A., Ph.D. — Pedigree of the English People, 16

Nicephorus Callistus — Historia Ecclesiastica, 139

O'Connor, C. — Dissertation on Irish History, 68

O'Curry, E. — Manners and Customs of the Ancient Irish, 52, 68

O'Driscoll, John — History of Ireland, 129

   ,,   ,, — Views of Ireland, 131

O'Mulconry — Irish Glossary, 52

Origen — Homily in Ezekiel, 59, 65

   ,, — Homily in Lucae, 91

Owen, William — Myvrian Archaeology, 20, 21, 48, 59

Oxford Icelandic Dictionary — 112, 113

Palgrave, Sir Francis — English Commonwealth, 16

   ,,   ,,   ,, — History of the Anglo-Saxons, 114

Parfitt, Canon — St. George of Merry England, 32

Paton, James — British History and Papal Claims, 119

Petrie, Dr. George — Tara Hill, 102

Petrie, Henry — Annales Cambriae, 60, 121, 122

Pezron — Antiq. de la Nation et de Langue Gaulaise, 16

Phillips, Dr. John — Yorks. Phil. Society, 29

Phlegon — Chronicles of the Olympiades, 68

Pliny — Natural History, 19, 67

Procopious — De Gothicis, 65

Rees, W. J. — Cambro-British Saints, 106

Reeves, Dr. W. — Vita Adamnan, 52, 67, 69, 107

   ,,   ,,   ,, — Vita Columbae, 102

   ,,   ,,   ,, — The Culdees, 129

Registrum Prioratus S. Andree — 126, 127, 133

Richardson, William — Godwin de Presulibus, 65, 87

Rolleston, Frances — Mazzaroth, 113

Sabellius apud Ennodius   94

Salvian   On the Government of God, 43

Saussaye, De la   La Revue Numismatique, 31

Schedius, Elias   Treatise de Mor. Germ, 63

Schöll, Carl William   Eccles. Brit. Scotor. Hist. Fontibus, 107

Senchus Mor. (Ancient Laws of Ireland)   25

Sismondi, Leonard de   Histoire des Francais, 147

Skene, W. Forbes   Four Ancient Books of Wales, 67

Smith, G., L.L.D.   Religions of Ancient Britain, 64, 95

Smith, J.   Galic Antiquities, 28, 53

,,   ,,   History of the Druids, 55

Snorre, Sturleson   Heimskringla, 113

Soames, Henry   Bampton Lectures, 92

Spartian   Vita Hadriani, 41

Spelman, Sir Henry   Concilia, 89, 90, 117

Spence, Magnus   Standing Stones of Stennes, 58

Spenser, Edmund   Faerie Queen, 21, 60

Stanihurst, Richard   De Rebus in Hibernia Gestis, 52

Stanley, Dean   Mem. of Westminster Abbey, 137

Stone, Gilbert   England from the Earliest Times, 16, 27

Strabo   Geography, 19, 26, 31, 50, 55, 60

Strype, Rev. John   Annals of the Reformation, 150

Stukeley, William   Abury, 24, 58, 63, 64

,,   ,,   Stonehenge, 54, 78

,,   ,,   Minutes of Antiq. Soc. London (1878), 28

Suetonius   Caligula, 38, 50

Tacitus   Annals, 34, 35, 37, 38, 39, 76, 77

,,   Vita Agricolae, 16, 42, 76, 77

Tertullian   Adversus Judaeos, 91, 100

Theodoret — Religious History, 138

Thierry, J. N. — Norman Conquest, 16

Tillemont. Seb. le Nain de — Histoire Ecclésiastique, 104

Tirechan — St. Patrick, 106

Toland, John — History of the Druids, 20, 50, 53, 72, 74, 96

Triads — 21, 37, 38, 48, 55, 61, 82, 93.

Turner, Sharon — History of the Anglo-Saxons, 48

Twysden, Sir Roger — Historia Anglican Scriptores, 140

Tynemouth, John of — Nova Legenda Anglie (ed. Horstmann), 88

Ussher, Archbishop — Brit. Eccles. Antiq. (1639), 93, 135, 138

Vallancey, Charles — Collectanea de Rebus Hibernicae, 59, 62, 67

Vaughan, Robert — Hengwrt M.S.S., 118

Vergil, Polydore — Anglica Historia, 90

Waddell, Prof. L. A. — Origin of Britons, Scots, and Anglo-Saxons, 14

Warren, F. E. — Liturgy and Ritual of the Celtic Church, 88, 103

Wilford, Francis — Asiatic Researches, 42

Williams, Edward — Iolo M.S.S., 88, 99, 105

Williams, H., D.D. — Christianity in Early Britain 126

Williams, Rev. Archdeacon — Gomer, 47

Wilson, Elizabeth — Lights and Shadows, 61, 62

Wright, T. — History of Scotland, 140

Wylie, Rev. J. A., LL.D. — History of Scotland, 13, 127

Yeatman, J. Pym — Early English History, 44

Zimmer, H. — The Celtic Church in Britain and Ireland, 107

Zonaras, Joannes — Annals, 39

Zozimus — Historia Nova, 27, 42

Zozomen — Historia Ecclesiasticae, 104

INDEX